INCOMES POLICY AND
CAPITAL SHARING
IN EUROPE

Derek Robinson

INCOMES POLICY
AND
CAPITAL SHARING
IN EUROPE

CROOM HELM LONDON

FIRST PUBLISHED 1973
© 1973 CHAPTER 2, 3, 4, 6 AND 8
OECD
© 1973 BY DEREK ROBINSON
CHAPTERS I, 5, AND 7

CROOM HELM LTD
2–10 ST JOHNS ROAD LONDON SW II

ISBN 0 85664–008–5

PRINTED IN GREAT BRITAIN
BY EBENEZER BAYLIS AND SON LTD
THE TRINITY PRESS, WORCESTER, AND LONDON
BOUND BY G. & J. KITCAT LTD, LONDON

CONTENTS

PREFACE

These papers were originally written for various international conferences or as reports of international study groups. Many of them were written for the OECD as part of the work of the Manpower and Social Affairs Directorate. This does not commit the OECD or the study group participants to the views expressed in the papers; these remain the responsibility of the author.

Some of the papers were written some time ago, but either they have been up-dated by the addition of sections covering more recent developments or it is considered that they are still of some relevance and interest today.

The first two chapters deal with incomes policies. Chapter 1 was written for an international conference on incomes policies held at Ditchley Park in 1971. Short sections have been added to describe more recent developments in some of the countries. Some of the implications for policy making drawn from Chapter 1 appear in Chapter 2. Chapter 2 began as a paper written for the OECD in 1970 and was amended slightly in the light of discussion.

The next section of papers are around the theme of schemes for the encouragement or provision of wealth assets for employed persons. Chapter 3 is a report of trade union experts on the general subject of capital-sharing. The meeting took place in December 1970. While the attitudes of one or two specific trade unions, or federations, may have changed a little from the views expressed at that meeting by their representatives, this does not affect the purpose of the paper which is, essentially, to provide a discussion of trade union attitudes on the level of general argument and principles, rather than to account for the views of any particular trade union. Chapter 4 is the report of a multi-national study group to the Federal Republic of Germany which took place in 1971. Chapter 5 consists of a background paper on the subject of capital-sharing. This is a composite document

1*

9

which has been used for general briefing purposes at a number of international conferences and study groups and reproduces an outline of the scheme for capital-sharing put forward by the Danish LO, the central trade union organisation, in 1970.

The third section is centred round the theme of collective bargaining. Chapter 6 is a report of trade union experts on the subject of bargaining with multi-national companies. The meeting was held in 1969. Chapter 7 was originally written for an International Conference on Industrial Relations held in Tel Aviv, 1971, and sought to raise some of the underlying issues of productivity bargaining. It is mainly concerned with the decision-taking and regulatory aspects. Chapter 8 was first written for an OECD seminar on manpower forecasting in 1970. It is based on surveys of the behaviour of labour markets in a number of European countries and seeks to present some of the experiences of how labour markets really function within a framework of market developments.

CHAPTER 1

Prices and Incomes Policies—Recent Developments in Some European Countries

Introduction

Prices and incomes policies have been discussed in Europe continuously since 1945. Different countries have, at some time or another, advocated some form of prices and/or incomes control. Frequently there have been indications of a pendulum approach; there have been swings to and from different degrees of emphasis which can be regarded as different sorts of policies or even as swings towards and against incomes policies. Sometimes the pendulum appears to be the result merely of the desire to implement a policy which differs from that currently advocated. Certainly there are signs that at any one time it is the perceived deficiencies and difficulties of an approach, be it one which is generally recognised as a prices and incomes policy or be it one of non-intervention, which provide the greater impetus to action. The deficiencies and difficulties of the alternative policies seem to be less clearly perceived until they too become the implemented policies.

The papers on prices and incomes policies presented here do not attempt to evaluate the success or otherwise of such policies. This is due to two main reasons. There has been relatively little discussion of this by the practitioners, although academics have made numerous contributions. Even if there had been discussion of the policies the conclusions would not necessarily be regarded as laying down irreversible guidelines or immutable limitations on future decision-taking. Collective bargaining—and incomes policy is seen frequently as a form and extension of collective bargaining—is motivated by expectations and hopes for the future. The fact that trade unions might not have achieved all their goals through ordinary or orthodox collective bargaining does not lead them to conclude that they should cease to use this approach. They may well believe and hope that they will have greater success in the future. So it is with incomes policies. The fact that past policies have not necessarily achieved all the objectives sought for them does not of itself lead one to conclude that they cannot succeed in the future. There may be reasons why prices and incomes policies are unlikely to succeed at any time, but these are separate to the mere assessment of past policies. Evidence from previous policy measures are relevant to a consideration of current and future policy decisions but it is a question of judgement how relevant they are, or what, exactly, the conclusions to be drawn from them should be.

Secondly, there is no general agreement about the criteria for judging the success of prices and incomes policies. The declared criteria, expounded when the policy is in operation, may be the true ones, but may also be in part one of the means of achieving the objectives. To the extent that a policy seeks to change people's behaviour and attitudes it is probably necessary to stress the advantages of the policy, and claim that it is successful, even when the tide of events may have begun to turn against it. For it is difficult to see how others can be persuaded to modify their behaviour if they are told that everyone else is failing to do so. The actual assessment of the results of a policy are also a matter of some debate. Essentially all methods rely on forecasting what would have happened in the absence of the policy. This is by its very nature a hazardous undertaking. Certainty is not possible. Moreover there are some signs that some of the assessments have relied on statistics and variables which have been selected not for their importance and relevance to the policy decisions underlying and comprising the prices and incomes policy but selected because of their availability, suitability for econometric analysis or because they provided an unbroken series. Some of the objectives of incomes policy might not be testable in any very precise way. Or if they are it might be only after the passing of time sufficiently long to permit the effects of the cycle to be removed from the immediate years under analysis. Thus, for example, the productivity-increasing pressure of the British policy in the period 1966–9 might not have emerged until the 1970s.

These papers are not therefore really concerned with testing the success or otherwise of prices and incomes policies. Nevertheless, one general comment will be made. It appears that prices and incomes policies are tested by much more rigorous criteria and standards than are other forms of policy such as fiscal or monetary policies. If an incomes policy does not stop all inflation there are cries made to abandon it on the grounds that it has obviously failed. If similar criteria were applied equally to all other policy measures most governments would be left completely defenceless with no policy measures whatever available to them. It is particularly noticeable that the criteria adopted by government decision-makers and advisers are much more realistic. They tend to judge according to whether things seem a little better with a particular policy than they would have been without it. This too requires some forecasting of what would have happened in different circumstances and this too is open to error. But as it is frequently done without claims for excessive accuracy and precision, in that the direction of the changes is considered and the magnitude regarded with appropriate qualifications, there is not the same blind acceptance of conclusions from the statistical analysis. At the same time, to ignore all factual evidence and disregard all statistical or econometric analysis would be as misguided as to place blind faith in all regression analysis. It is necessary to exercise judgement about what weight to attach to various pieces of evidence as well as to what is actually evidence. Any policy that rests for much of its success on changing people's attitudes must be a somewhat imprecise affair.

The central theme of the papers presented here is how to decide whether a prices and incomes policy is possible, given the objectives and preferences of the various parties. It is centred round the problems of actually applying a policy and the different ways, methods and techniques that have been adopted in different countries to give effect to agreed objectives. It reflects the writer's belief that a successful voluntary prices and incomes policy requires that trade unions be satisfied that they can continue to work towards their objects in ways considered suitable to them. Without this, it is argued, any long-term policy must fail. Trade unions are taken as the more important party because they have the obvious power to prevent an incomes policy in most of the countries studied, or at least, have so, as long as employers continue to behave in the same sort of way that they have hitherto.

It is not intended to cover all European countries, or even all those which might claim to have a prices and incomes policy. The selection has been determined by two factors; either there have been some recent changes which are considered sufficiently interesting to merit discussion, or, as in the case of Austria, the general arrangements are thought to be worth describing because they have not been widely considered elsewhere. This approach means that some countries are not included, e.g. Norway. However reference can be made to the OECD report *Inflation* which in addition to general analysis of the problems of prices and incomes policies contains summaries of recent developments in selected countries.

This paper is descriptive rather than analytical, although there are comments on the nature of some of the problems arising in the countries concerned which are to some extent relevant to other countries. It is stressed however that the particular institutions, traditions and type of arrangements existing in different countries mean that great caution has to be exercised when seeking to carry the lessons of one country to another. In particular the attitudes of governments, trade unions and employers vary considerably, and it is suggested that essentially incomes policy is a question of attitudes.

Austria

There has been a tradition of voluntary co-operation in the prices and incomes field in Austria going back to the end of the war. The economic conditions resulting from the war and the occupation encouraged voluntary co-operation. In addition the traditional organisations of Chambers for Trade and Industry, Labour and Agriculture, whereby all members of the appropriate Chamber must subscribe to the finance of these organisations, had led to the practice of centralised decision-taking and discussion. In 1957 the Joint Commission on Prices and Wages was established with representatives of government and the three major Chambers. The Trade Union Federation also had members so that there was, in fact, a parity between the trade unions and employers. The original objective of the

Commission was to influence the trend of prices and wages and this still remains its main activity, although a sub-commission also discusses general economic development. The participation is voluntary and there are no legal sanctions to enforce the views of the Commission. Discussion covers a broad range of social and economic policy as well as specific wage and price movements. Initially the emphasis was on prices for which a joint sub-committee was established. In 1962 a similar joint sub-committee on wages was set up. At the end of 1963 a third body, the Capital Advisory Council on Economic and Social Problems, was also established.

The Sub-Committee on Prices

There are six members, one from each of the four major organisations of the social partners and from the Ministry of Interior and the Ministry of Finance. The committee meets weekly and the chair is taken by the Federal Chamber of Industry and Commerce. Proposals from individual firms or sectors of industry to raise prices are submitted first to the Federal Chamber of Commerce and Industry which then passes them on to the joint sub-committee. The sub-committee may agree unanimously to refer the proposal back or submit it to the Joint Commission for approval. In practice the prices subjected to this form of control are restricted to branded articles, staple commodities and standardised services. These represent about 20 per cent of the consumer price index. In addition, a further 25 per cent of the consumer price index goods can be influenced directly by the provisions of the price control laws. The general guiding principle governing the decisions of the joint sub-committee is that price increases are justified only if substantial cost increases have occurred. It is necessary, therefore, that applications for price increases should indicate how costs have risen but this is generally done on a rather rough calculation taking into account the changes which have occurred in the costs of labour and raw materials based upon their relative proportions of overall costs. On the whole management does not submit detailed figures. Factors such as the degree of capacity utilisation, the improvements in productivity, or the market position of the firms are seldom taken into account, therefore. In principle the Minister of

Interior has the power to fix an official price for a six-monthly period where the firm concerned controls the market. This power has not been applied. It would require the unanimous agreement of all four organisations.

The Sub-Commission on Wages

The committee is composed only of representatives of management and labour. It meets fortnightly, the chair being taken alternatively by a representative of the Trade Union Federation and the Federal Chamber of Industry and Commerce. Decisions have to be unanimous. If no decision has been reached after six weeks the issue is referred to the Joint Commission which has a further five weeks within which to reach a decision. If after this time no decision has been reached, collective bargaining may begin. The Raab-Benya agreement of 1963 accepted in principle that wherever possible the deadline for handling wage claims should not be implemented.

A trade union proposing to open wage negotiations notifies the trade union Federation which applies to the joint sub-committee on wages for permission to formally open the negotiations. The trade union Federation is therefore in some position to influence the application before it reaches the joint sub-committee. This allows some degree of co-ordination of tactics within the Federation. The Federation is able to exert some influence on the timing of wage claims and possibly in certain extreme cases upon the actual size of the claim. The extent to which the Federation may seek to or succeed in influencing the size of a wage claim is not perfectly clear. The general impression is that it does not overtly seek to do so. If there is no agreement within the joint sub-committee or if it is regarded as being of fundamental importance, or if there is the likelihood of a price increase resulting from the wage claim, the application to open bargaining can be passed on to the full Joint Commission. The Joint Commission and the sub-committee cannot exert direct overt influence on the content of the wage agreements but it appears likely that because of the procedures and its rules of operation it has some scope for slowing down wage settlements and *possibly* for influencing the ultimate outcome.

Advisory Council on Economic and Social Problems

The committee stemmed from the acceptance of the view that the general slowing down in growth rates and the tendency for inflation to increase which were noted towards the end of the 50's and the 60's necessitated some research into the state of the Austrian economy and solutions for its improvement. It was apparent that for such policies to be produced and implemented there would need to be a minimum of agreement between the social partners and the government. It was, therefore, in some ways a logical development of the Joint Price Wage Commission and its sub-committee that this third joint committee should be established.

The Advisory Council represents the major organisations of the social partners as well as the professional or technical research experts. While the need to secure agreement may in some ways slow down the purely technical aspects of the Council's work this is perhaps more than counterbalanced by the fact that when results do emerge they have already secured a considerable amount of agreement and support from the social partners. Thus there is a tendency for agreed solutions or positions to emerge from the discussions of the Advisory Council. It is more difficult, therefore, for fundamentally different alternative policies to be publicly discussed. However, the organisation of the social partners is such that discussion of alternative analyses and solutions takes place before the Advisory Council's ultimate report.

A notable feature is the degree of co-operation and joint analysis that is reflected in the work of these organisations. This does not mean that the parties have an identity of view any more than they have an identity of interests, but they do appear to have developed organisations which allow them to discuss their different views and objectives in such a way that generally agreed solutions are often forthcoming. To a considerable extent this is much helped by the great overlapping and interlocking of relatively few key personnel in the various organisations. Individuals meet each other frequently on a number of different committees and commissions. They get to know each other and each other's points of view and they are able to re-enforce their decisions on any one committee or commission by their decisions and actions on other bodies. In particular the exchange of personnel and the overlapping of functionaries in the trade union Federation and the Chamber of Labour and equally on the employer's side means that the voluntary mechanisms and the statutorily provided mechanisms are very often operated by the same personnel. There seems to be a qualitative aspect of the organisations and the way in which they operate which cannot be understood merely from a study of the formal organisations.

There is no official claim that a prices and incomes policy exists in Austria. Rather there is the view that there is some form of agreement at national level between workers and employers and their representatives and government. There are no guideposts and no criteria for incomes policy. The processes are regarded as being a constant constructive dialogue between government and the social partners on a wide range of economic issues. The trade unions would be reluctant to describe these arrangements as an incomes policy for they are not thought to cover all forms of incomes. It is very clear that both social partners believe that they are in a position to influence government social and economic policy and because of this belief are willing to take part in discussions which influence directly wages and prices. It is not easy to establish precisely the degree of influence that is exerted by the joint commissions and it is not possible to quantify this. It would appear that the influence on wages has been more on the timing of wage increases although it is likely that informal discussions within the trade union Federation have also influenced the size of some wage claims or settlements. On the prices side the control has probably been more direct and effective although one result may well have been to ensure that price increases for certain commodities take place at the same point in time.

Wage Bargaining

There are differences in approach between the different trade unions regarding wage bargaining. This can perhaps be illustrated by the examples of the metal workers union and the food workers union. The metal workers union seeks a central settlement that provides a minimum basis. Trade unions at plant level may then seek to obtain additional increases according to the economic circumstances of their company. The food industry on the other hand prefers to negotiate on narrower sectional fronts rather than have one large central agreement. These agreements tend to go for relatively higher wage settlements but there is no second stage negotiation at plant or company level.

The overall effects of these two approaches seem not to be terribly different as there have been no marked changes in relative wages between the various sectors over the past few years. It therefore seems that the two-stage bargaining of the metal workers leads to a general movement in earnings in percentage terms much in line with that received by the narrower based one-stage bargaining in the food industry.

It is typical in a number of agreements that those receiving only the minimum wage as set out in the contract receive larger percentage increases than those who are receiving higher pay. This is an attempt to prevent internal differentials from widening. As there does not appear to be any marked changes in differentials within industries it would appear that this is essentially in practice a status quo solution. It does not seem that there are any marked changes in the distribution of earnings within an industry. Plant level wage negotiations are excluded from scrutiny of the joint wages sub-committee. Equally only wage increases resulting from the national settlement are taken into account on the joint prices sub-committee when considering requests for price increases.

In some sectors there are a number of collective agreements with different dates. The joint wage sub-committee may delay some of the applications to reopen bargaining on some of these contracts in order that a number of them can be negotiated at the same time. Similarly certain groups may be excluded from particular negotiations.

The importance of the fast rate of economic growth in allowing the Trade Union Federation and the Joint Wage Sub-Committee to exercise delays upon some wage claims cannot be over-emphasised. It is because real incomes are growing that trade unions and their members are prepared to accept this form of intervention. And they are able to reinforce their decisions on any one committee or commission by their decisions and actions on other bodies.

Summary of Wage Behaviour

1. There is no official guidelines policy but constant contact at trade union level, formally and informally, means that there is some consensus of opinion about the possible wage developments that are consistent with the goals of the economy.

2. Such a policy is seen in a long-term setting although the short-term aspects of it may reflect the current economic situation.

3. This approach is integrated with broad and deep discussions on economic policy so that objectives may be reached either directly by wage bargaining or by some other form, e.g. budgetary measures introduced by the government in response to trade union pressure.

4. There is a view that wage and price decisions should be taken openly and in public, although it may be that the Austrian experience appears to suggest that schemes might well work better if they are taken privately, i.e. at informal meetings.

Prices

On the prices side it appears that different sectors of activity are affected in different ways. The price policy impinges most heavily on those sectors producing branded or standardised products. Sectors where there are frequent product changes may feel less weight from the policy. The price control aspects apply only to a change in price; the price of a new product is not subject to the influence of the Joint Price Sub-Committee. It is possible that created product changes may be regarded as a new product and therefore not subject to scrutiny.

There is some possibility that price restraint may lead to a shortage of internally-provided funds for some companies which could have an adverse effect on self-financed investment. Whether this will have a deleterious effect on the total amount of investment, or on the direction and allocation of investment funds will depend in part at least upon the possibilities of obtaining externally-provided funds.

Prices of imported goods are not subject to price scrutiny.

This will probably mean that an increasing proportion of total products will be exempted as the volume of imports rises or as the imported content increases. Prices of this category of goods will exert an influence on the prices of similar products manufactured in Austria.

Particular Features of the Austrian Situation

1. The initiative for the machinery and the organisation came from the two social partners themselves. They were not imposed from above by government in an attempt to obtain certain wage-price or demand management policies. The parties themselves sought to establish frequent means of effective co-operation for their mutual benefit. Wage and price policy is not seen as being essentially a part of demand management policy imposed upon reluctant social partners by a government which seeks some additional weapon in its armoury.

2. This leads to a second important conclusion—the Austrian trade unions believe that they are able to influence social and economic policies of government. Their actions in the wage and prices field are seen merely as a part of total economic policy, all of which affects their members' interests and all of which they believe is capable to some degree or other of adjustment in response to trade union pressures. There is in a sense a trade-off between complete unilateral or bilateral action in the wage and price field and the securing of desired social and economic policies from government. This means that any wage or price moderation is not seen as impinging unduly upon the social partners' freedom of action but rather as a part of a generally agreed and in some ways co-ordinated approach to social and economic policies.

This is not to imply that there are no differences between the two social partners in their social and economic policy nor that there are no differences between them, either collectively or individually, and government. Rather there is a general consensus or there is a belief that it is possible to produce a general consensus which implies on occasions giving as well as taking so that wage and price policy should be seen merely as one facet of a very wide range of social and economic policies.

3. It is perhaps for this reason that the wage and price policy is essentially a qualitative rather than a quantitative policy.

Any wage-price or income policy must choose between a basically qualitative or quantitative approach. A qualitative approach we would take to mean something like a guidelines policy. There would be an attempt to lay down or agree upon general norms and possibly exception clauses but essentially the policy would seek to restrain wage increases to some pre-determined numerical quantity. While there may be some unwritten, indeed perhaps even unstated, general view as to what the economy can stand in quantitative terms for wage and price increases, the policy itself does not operate in a quantitative framework. Decisions do not have to conform to some specific numerical guideline. It is, therefore, easier to reach agreement provided, as always, that there is a genuine basic desire to reach agreement.

Finland

Recent Developments[1]

After what was generally regarded as a poor economic performance followed by devaluation there was a widespread acceptance of the view that some urgent and new approach to economic policy was necessary. There was a realisation that an economic state of emergency existed.[2] This changed climate permitted as well as demanded changes in economic behaviour.

A Stabilisation Agreement was signed by unions and employers in March, 1968. The practice of indexation, previously widespread, was ended in all parts of the economy including price contracts. The general increase in wages was to be about the same as the increase in productivity, i.e. 3–4 per cent. However, the wage increases were not to be granted in percentage form but by a flat-rate increase of 16 pennies an hour (equal to 3·5 per cent). As part of the general agreement, there were to be controls on prices and rents, and government was to control agricultural prices and thus incomes. The

---

[1] This section is taken from a paper written in mid-1970. Later developments are discussed at the end of the Finnish section.

[2] The term "state of emergency" was used by everyone I talked to.

practice of central settlements covering blue-collar workers in the private sector was already established.

A Prices and Wages Council was established on a tripartite basis. The wages section has not met. The prices section adopted the general principle that wage increases were not to be permitted grounds for price increases although exceptions were made for labour intensive industries and the service sector.

In September, 1969, a Second Stabilisation Agreement was agreed. The wage increase was in two parts; firstly, a general flat-rate increase of 18 pennies an hour or by one per cent should the 18 pennies an hour increase be less than one per cent, and secondly, a further increase of one per cent to be allocated in wage increases as the social partners in each sector or branch decided.

Civil service salaries were to be increased accordingly by law.

Working of the Agreements

Essentially the agreements covered wages and salaries negotiated by the labour market organisations, prices, excluding imported products, and agricultural incomes as determined by government agricultural policy. The government exercised its influence in the two Stabilisation Agreements through the person of the then State Arbitrator. His task was to obtain a central settlement that would not be inflationary, and to do this it was necessary for him to enter discussion with the social partners on a wider range of economic issues.

Once the Agreements were made any additional wage increases came as a result of wage drift. There were some unofficial wildcat strikes for higher wages, and it is understood that the central employers' organisation, STK, advised their members in these situations not to grant increases, in an attempt to prevent wage drift spreading. There was considerable discussion, and some disagreement, as to how much of the increase in earnings over and above that resulting from the central settlement was due to structural changes in the economy and how much to wage drift proper.

Price control was fairly comprehensive under the First Agreement but modified a little under the Second. It is understood that some 70 per cent of the cost-of-living index is covered by price control. Prices are frozen at the levels existing on some particular date, as are profit margins and retailers' margins. Any customer can complain to the price inspectorate that prices have been improperly increased. If the complaint is found justified, fines can be levied in relation to the improper profit made. The central organisations of employers, both the labour market and the industrial and commercial organisations, support the price policy and expect their members to observe it. This is a crucial consideration, as it means that individual firms who break the policy cannot expect support from their own organisations.

Imports are excluded from control as are a number of semi-finished products. It was thought that control over the final price would exercise some restraining action as purchasers would refuse to pay higher prices for bought-in components, but it is understood that this has not proved to be so in practice.

It is widely agreed by both social partners that the central wage settlements would not have been possible without the price controls. This is why the STK supports it, although it would prefer to see some gradual relaxation. In principle, therefore, there is agreement on the interdependence of wage and price restraint and an acceptance that the controls on prices can, and must, be more strict than those on wages.

Wage drift has occurred in certain sectors. Different estimates of drift were given by different organisations, but it seems that during 1969 it might have been of the order of 2–3 per cent at least. It is accepted that some drift is inevitable, but the consequences of drift within a central settlement that imposes fairly strict limits on non-drift sectors are increasingly felt.

Problems Emerging

1. *Wage drift.* The non-drift sectors are pressing for some form of compensation for their relatively lower rates of increase. This is a problem with all central settlements and all incomes policies that do not prevent all wage drift completely. Difficulties will arise over the question of how much of the increases are "drift proper" and how much are increases in earnings reflecting structural changes in the economy as a result of shifts of labour between occupations, branches or resulting

from higher output. Differences of opinion and different policy positions will probably be adopted by the two trade union organisations, the white-collar TVK and the blue-collar SAK, and it is also possible that differences will emerge within the SAK.

The employers recognise that drift will probably increase as the labour market becomes tighter as a result of continued economic growth, although the continued prosperity might ease the labour market position a little by reducing or even reversing the flow of labour to Sweden. They are also realistic in recognising that relatively low central settlements will always be subject to pressure from drift as employers compete for labour and workers realise they can obtain increases by local pressure.

2. *Flat-rate or percentage increases.* The First Agreement was flat-rate and the Second a mixture. Pressures are building up, particularly in the TVK and among some of the skilled blue-collar unions to have percentage increases, while part of the SAK wishes to see flat-rate increases on the grounds of solidarity. It is possible that the trade union organisations could not agree to a settlement that was completely flat-rate. Employers prefer percentage increases but not to the point of jeopardising the Agreement. This issue emphasises the institutional pressures operating on a trade union organisation with this sort of policy. Different groups of workers react differently to measures which change traditional differentials. The white-collar unions feel particularly strongly about this, as they see their differentials narrowed in two ways, by flat-rate settlements and by wage drift increases received by other groups which are not open to them.

As the economy improves and the sense of emergency diminishes, groups of workers will be decreasingly prepared to see a worsening of their own relative position unless they are convinced on some other grounds that such a change is desirable. This can sometimes happen; e.g. skilled workers might if special measures are taken to help the lower-paid workers, but is unlikely to happen for white-collar in respect of blue-collar workers generally. The basis of the increase is not only the most important area of dispute; it is the one that could prevent a Third Agreement.

All three labour market organisations—STK, SAK, and TVK—appear to favour some degree of flexibility in the next settlement which would permit some degree of compensation to be given to non-drift sectors and perhaps allow a branch or sector to allocate a given increase in its total wage and salary bill in some slightly different way. The attempts to provide this flexibility will subject the Stabilisation Agreements to possibly their stiffest test so far.

3. *Coverage of policy*. The trade unions are increasingly concerned that the Stabilisation Agreements, even when reinforced by the price controls, do not cover all incomes. There are some non-wage incomes, e.g. profits and some agricultural and forestry, which they believe are escaping control, in total or part, and they are concerned to bring these incomes under control on two grounds. Firstly, on social grounds of equity of treatment and equity of control and sacrifice. Secondly, on economic grounds that as the economy expands and prosperity increases, it will not be sufficient to try and exercise adequate economic control merely through the existing Stabilisation Agreements and price control, as the economy will require more broadly-based instruments of control. Employers and other groups will resist this extension as they will resist the extension of the policy to other areas of economic activity, e.g. the distribution of income between wages and profits. It is probable, therefore, that the unity of purpose of the last two years will be subjected to increasing pressures which could destroy it. There are certain conflicts of interest and objective between the two social partners, although of course there are many points of similar interest, too; and these conflicts will emerge more strongly as the economy improves. The voluntary deposits of profits in the central bank by companies might come under increasingly hostile scrutiny by trade unions.

Conclusions

There is little doubt that Finland has been successful in restraining the increase in money wages in the last two years. The policy was introduced in a period of economic emergency that was recognised as such by the general public. This meant that there was a tremendous fund of good will towards the policies and a great willingness to co-operate and exercise restraint. The economy is now improving and there are considerable improvements in real income, some 5–6 per cent p.a. in 1969 and 1970. The fund of goodwill may well be diminishing at a rapid pace. Already there appear to be some differences of opinion between rank and file members of trade unions and some of the national leadership. As the sense of emergency is reduced, the rank and file become impatient for some of the fruits of their past sacrifices. Trade union leadership, on the other hand, may appreciate that incomes policy is essentially a long-term operation: "It is investing in growth and that means investing in the future."

This is a built-in conflict. In order to obtain the immediate support of rank and file, it is necessary to emphasise the emergency nature of the problems. In order to obtain the full benefits of the policy, it is necessary to take a long-term view. The emergency is seen as short-term, and thus conflicts with the underlying long-term objectives. This conflict exists in the attempts of most countries to establish a prices and incomes policy.

In addition institutional pressures are now emerging in Finland. Different groups of workers want different sorts of policy. Trade unions in some sectors find it much more difficult to accept a freeze situation as implied by the central settlement. For example, a central settlement freezes bad agreements as well as good ones so that sectors newly organised by trade unions feel they are being unfairly held back; and they may feel the need to obtain particularly good settlements in order to retain an increase in membership.

Political pressures are emerging; as the Stabilisation Agreements are seen to have important economic consequences, it is clear that attitudes towards them will be affected by political positions.

As the economy improves the central settlement or any settlement that leads to lower money wage increases than would occur without the policy will be subject to increasing pressures. Rank and file trade unionists will see that they can obtain higher money wages than those negotiated by their trade union. Employers will increasingly be tempted to bid up wages as they compete for ever-scarcer labour. Industrial and political opponents of trade union leadership will be able to make attacks on the "failure" of unions to obtain the highest money increases and the leadership may find it increasingly difficult to argue in terms of "real increases" or long-term effects for the sense of emergency will be constantly reduced. The next two or three years are, therefore, the most testing time for the Finnish policy; for while it is subjected to these pressures, it is probable that the trade unions will seek to change the policy from one of Stabilisation of wages and prices to a full incomes policy in the widest sense, which will be part of a comprehensive approach to the major social and economic issues of the day.

The Third Agreement

A Third Agreement on labour and economic policy was signed in December, 1970, but significantly it was not signed by the white-collar trade union Federation. It proved much more difficult to reach agreement on this occasion and the President of the Republic intervened in order to urge the two parties to reach agreement. He presented a package of proposals to them and emphasised that his proposals were a complete package to be accepted or rejected as a whole. He proposed that price controls should be continued in their existing form while recognising that some of the proposed wage increases might, of necessity, lead to increased prices in some cases.

Profits in the timber sector had been growing at an unusually fast rate which had led to dissatisfaction amongst the trade unions. The President included in his proposals a statement that he would submit a Counter Cyclical Tax Bill to Parliament. The tax would be imposed on the exports of the woodworking industries and be made retrospective to 1st September, 1969. The tax would be at the rate of 2·5 per cent of the value of wood products exported during that period. The funds accruing from this tax would be used to accelerate structural changes in employment, provide a wider diversification of production, and safeguard employment during the period of slower economic growth. Three-fifths of the fund could be used to finance residential building construction in localities where a housing shortage has retarded industrial expansion.

A universal minimum wage to be agreed by the parties was seen as providing some element of social justice and thereby satisfied some of the trade union demands. The President drew attention to the narrowing of differentials between the earnings of blue-collar and white-collar workers and the Civil Service and stated that this narrowing of the gap had been healthy for society as a whole. The SAK and STK had reached agreement on improvements in fringe benefits with the exception of changes in holidays. In order to break the deadlock the President announced that he intended to introduce legislation establishing a universal four-week holiday operative from 1973.

The wage agreement signed by the two social partners provided for a minimum hourly earnings for normal working hours of 3 Fmk. an hour for every able-bodied employee aged 18 or over. Benefits in kind are to be included in this figure. Direct wage increases are to be granted in two forms and at two dates. Over the full length of the agreement wages are to be increased by 0.42 Fmk. per hour plus an increase of 2 per cent of the total wage bill in each sector but with the allocation of this 2 per cent determined on a sector or branch basis. Agreements signed at sector or branch level after the signing of the central agreement can raise earnings by 0·22 Fmk. an hour plus the 2 per cent on an industry basis. It is possible for an industry to reduce the flat rate increase of 0·22 Fmk. per hour and arrange for a general percentage increase of 3 per cent on an industry or branch basis. The second phase of the agreement operates from 1st September, 1971, when earnings shall rise by a further 0·20 Fmk. an hour. The agreement is to run until the end of March, 1972.

The central wage agreement is thus a combination of flat rate and percentage increases which permits the sector or branch to increase the bias towards percentage-based increases if it so desires. This is an attempt to contain the various pressures resulting from the changes in differentials that have resulted from the first two stabilisation agreements. However, the white-collar workers have not signed the agreement, and it looks as though the metal workers, a strong trade union which did not fully accept the implications of the second stabilisation agreement, might continue to press for large wage increases in the metal-working industry. To the extent that they are successful, they may well jeopardise the Third Agreement.

In addition to the wage agreement the STK and SAK signed

an agreement on social benefits and other arrangements. They pledged themselves to jointly attempt to persuade the State and the Bank of Finland to increase State loans for the construction of houses for rent. In addition the STK recommends its member companies, when considering new investments, to bear in mind the need of housing for employees at new places of work.

They also stressed the need for rapid action to ease the transition of unemployed workers. A feature of the Finnish provisions is that the only persons who can be entered in unemployment registers are those whose health is insufficient for heavy manual labour. The parties are urging that action be taken to increase vocational training and improve the opportunities for re-employment. The agreement also provided for certain specific items of information to be given in confidence to the chief shop steward of a plant to enable him to be satisfied that the wage agreements were being properly applied. Employers agreed that shop stewards appointed by trade unions should have the same right as a statutory shop steward has by law to inspect the lists of overtime and emergency work and of the extra pay granted for such work. The chief shop steward is to be entitled to inspect the pricing systems in force for piece-work rates and the rules for fixing and calculating extra wages according to the circumstances followed under different systems of payment.

Latest Developments[3]

The 1970 agreement expired in March 1972 and was followed by a further central agreement to last for twelve months. This provided for a flat-rate increase of 0·25 Fmk. an hour plus an additional 3 per cent to be distributed as the negotiators in each sector decide. This 3 per cent "flexibility" increase can be increased to 4 per cent if the negotiators at industry level decide to transfer an equivalent part of the flat-rate 25 pennis for this purpose. Thus the central agreement once more reflects the conflicting pressure for flat-rate increases to narrow differentials and improve the position of the lower-paid with the desire of the more skilled workers and the white-collar workers to at

---

[3] Additional comments written in early 1973.

least maintain if not widen differentials. This has led to a two-tier type increase, plus the possibility of switching part of the flat-rate element if that should be decided. The tremendous pressures urging the central bargainers to provide a greater degree of flexibility for the industry or sector-level negotiators to modify the central settlement to suit their own requirements is a marked feature of Finnish development. The provision of "flexibility" possibilities is, of course, in keeping with the Scandinavian practices of collective bargaining, but also has the advantage that the central settlement does not create the feeling amongst industry-level bargainers that they are redundant. There are still tasks of wage bargaining to perform with a "flexibility" element.

The low paid received additional assistance as the minimum wage was increased by 9½ per cent. Overall average wage rates are expected to rise by about 7 per cent, and wage drift will probably cause this to lead to an increase in average earnings of about 11 per cent.

Some interesting work on the effects of prices and incomes policies in Finland has been carried out by Dr. Molander of the Research Institute of the Finnish Economy.[4] These results seem to establish that during the period 1968–71 the policy had significant effects in reducing inflationary pressures. Both money wage rates and consumer prices would have risen faster without a policy, but real wages rose faster than if they would have without a policy. Thus the restraint in money wages did not lead to restraint in real wages but rather to a faster rate of growth. However, non-wage incomes seem to have grown more quickly than they would have without a policy and to have done so to a greater extent than wages. Thus the share of wages in national income fell during 1969 and 1970 and fell not only in relation to the "expected" non-policy ratio, but also in actual percentage terms. Wages as a proportion of national income fell from about 49 per cent in early 1968 to a low of 47 per cent in the last quarter of 1969, recovering sharply in

---

[4] See *The Implications of Different Incomes Policies* and *The Input-output framework as part of a macro-economic model: production-price income block in the bank of Finland Quarterly Econometric Model*, Halttunen and Molander (both mimeo.).

1971 so that it was a little over 50 per cent by the fourth quarter. This redistribution of income away from wages towards profits aroused the trade unions and is one of the explanations of the much tougher negotiating positions adopted by the unions. Their hostility was, at a general level, a reflection of their discontent with the redistributory effects of the prices and incomes policy (although the Finns would refer to this as a stabilisation policy and not an incomes policy as some incomes were excluded or subject to different and possibly weaker forms of control) and, at a particular level, because of the changes in wage differentials and relativities.

The new approach to policy included the creation of machinery specifically designed to co-ordinate the actions of the various labour market and product market partners. An Information Committee was set up to discuss developments and try to interpret the specific policy requirements of general policy statements.

To summarise, over the period March 1968 to December 1970 the increase in the cost of living was kept down to an annual rate of about 2·2 per cent. This was the result of the existence of statutory powers but owed more to the co-operation of government, trade unions and employers, and their determination to exert strong restraining pressure on inflationary tendencies. During 1971 inflation was about 8½ per cent and probably only slightly lower in 1972. The machinery of the stabilisation programme was maintained, in modified ways, particularly with regard to the tripartite relationships which were placed on a more continuing basis, and it was hoped that greater success might be achieved in 1973 than the two earlier years. The desire to make the policy work receded with the immediate experiences of devaluation in 1967. At the same time it is probably true to claim that the central fiscal and monetary authorities exerted less stringent general demand management controls in 1971 and 1972. The price increases emanating externally injected inflationary pressures into the Finnish economy and it may be that in some ways parts of the policy were too effective. As the incomes of some primary producers rose as a result of increases in world prices, their profits rose thereby distorting the distribution of income between factors. If there has been less control over wages in this period this redistribution might have been less and thus less pressure might have been subsequently exerted to restore some previous ratios.

Ireland

The Irish Government has been increasingly concerned about wage inflation and subsequent increases in unit labour costs. It would appear that to some extent the Irish wage increases are matching those of the U.K. although the level of productivity is lower. Therefore the out-turn of unit labour costs is particularly disadvantageous. Towards the end of 1970 the Government proposed to introduce a statutory prices and incomes policy. This was strongly opposed by both employers and trade unions who subsequently signed an "Employer-Labour Conference National Agreement" on the 21st December, 1970. In response to this the Government withdrew its proposals for a statutory policy.

The Agreement opened by stating that the two sides of industry agreed that: (a) It is essential that the rate of increase in costs and prices be moderated substantially; (b) all possible measures should be taken to ensure improvements in efficiency to offset increases in costs and charges so that increases in incomes represent real increases; (c) industrial peace must prevail to achieve these objectives.

Collective bargaining in Ireland follows the Wage Round in a much more formalised method than in most countries. However, while the general range of increases in each particular Round is related, the timing is such that increases under each Round do not appear in close proximity to each other. Thus increases under the last Wage Round, the Twelfth Round, will not be received by all workers until well into 1971. Accordingly the provisions of this national Agreement take place after the increases due under the Twelfth Round have been received and therefore the timing of the provisions of the Agreement will vary from sector to sector.

The Agreement covered a period of eighteen months commencing on the termination date of the current agreement. All adult male employees received an increase of £2 per week at the commencement of the Agreement. Female adult workers

2

also received an increase of £2 where equal pay existed and 85 per cent of the increase in other cases. Twelve months after the commencement of the provisions of the National Agreement a second increase of 4 per cent may be applied to all basic wages and salaries. In addition a cost of living escalator clause is attached to the second phase, i.e. to operate twelve months after the commencement of the Agreement. For each 1 per cent increase in the consumer price index over an increase of 4 per cent in the year covered by the first phase, an increase of three shillings (15 p.) a week shall be added to the 4 per cent wage increase then due. Thus, any increase in the consumer price index over 4 per cent which takes place in the first twelve months of the new Agreement will be compensated for after this date. The Agreement provided that trade unions shall not enter a strike or other form of industrial action in support of claims for increases in excess of the above amounts. The increases in pay are to be negotiated at industry or company level and the two sides are to have regard to the ability of particular industries or companies to absorb any increases in labour without impairing their competitive position or viability. The two parties to the Agreement are to meet in January 1972 to review the terms and operation of the Agreement although this implies no commitment to alter either the period covered or to vary its terms.

This might be seen as the first step by trade unions and employers collectively to secure some general agreement on the movement in money wages. It was conducted under the threat of Government statutory intervention. The Agreement sought to handle the question of differentials by providing that the first phase increase would be a flat rate increase while the second phase was in percentage terms. The overall result will be therefore to reduce differentials as the flat rate amount is greater than the percentage increase. There are signs that the Agreement is already being threatened by particular groups, e.g. airline workers, but nevertheless, it may be that this first hesitant and perhaps reluctant step towards general agreement on wage movement could provide some basis for the ultimate creation of a more far-reaching prices and incomes policy.

The Second National Agreement, 31 July 1972[5]

As we have seen, the First National Agreement provided for increases to last for twelve months followed by a second stage increase, but the date of implementation of the first rise was left to the parties to negotiate in accordance with their usual bargaining practices. There was no common starting date; each bargaining unit, at industry or firm level, negotiated its own agreement within the framework of the National Agreement and at such time as was proper following the staggered settlements received under the previous loose arrangements of the Wage Round.

A Second National Agreement was signed on 31st July, 1972. As with the First National Agreement, wage increases were to be received in two phases. The first phase, to operate for twelve months from the date of negotiation of the industry or firm-level settlement, provided for a 9 per cent increase on the first £30 of basic pay, or £2·50 for adult males and £2·25 for adult females, whichever was the larger; increases of 7½ per cent on the next £10 of basic pay and 4 per cent on any remaining pay were provided to taper off the general increase. Moreover in order to protect the real value of the increases received by those sectors settling relatively late in the period covered, certain specified additions were payable. For example, where settlements took place in the period 1st July, 1972–31st December, 1972, an extra 10 p. a week was payable from 1st January, 1973 and a second 10 p. a week from 1st July, 1973. Where settlement took place between 1st January, 1973–30th June, 1973, the first extra 10 p. was due on the date of the settlement and the second on 1st July, 1973. One effect of these provisions is to raise the "guaranteed" increase of £2·50 for men and £2·25 for females to £2·70 and £2·45 in those cases where the increases receivable under the national agreement were not translated into industry of firm-level settlements until 1st July, 1972.

The second phase of the agreement which became operative twelve months after the settlement arrived at under phase 1,

---

[5] This section is an addendum to the original paper, written to describe the subsequent developments.

provided for an increase of 4 per cent of basic wages and salaries. In addition a cost of living escalator provision gave an extra 16 p. a week for every 1 per cent increase in the Consumer Price Index, over 4 per cent in the year covered by phase 1. Thus the principle of a threshold agreement with a time-lag dimensions was again incorporated into the National Agreement.

There was some modification of the flat-rate principle of the First National Agreement. The percentage increases were tapered according to income level and a "guaranteed" flat rate increase of £2·50 (or £2·70) for men was established to increase the tapering effect. As with experience in other countries, for example, Finland, the institutional pressure resulting from a rigid application of flat-rate increases exerted considerable influence on negotiators.

If national framework agreements are to continue it is obvious that a greater degree of standardisation in the timing of settlements made under them is desirable. The Second Agreement made some steps towards this by shortening the length of some settlements made under the 1970 Agreement. These settlements were intended to run for eighteen months, but those terminating after 31st March, 1973 and before 30th June, 1973 could be shortened by one month and those terminating after 30th June, 1973 by two months. Thus all settlements made under the December, 1970 National Agreement which were not actually operative until after September, 1971 are not required to run for the full eighteen months as laid down in the original First Agreement. The Second Agreement also contained a clause establishing a committee on terminal dates which "shall consider the existing agreements and shall make recommendations".[6] No criteria or guidelines for this committee were laid down but it seems quite clear from the context that it is intended to move yet further towards more standardised termination dates.

The Agreement contained fairly detailed provisions about moves towards equal pay, laying down circumstances in which preferential increases could be given to females and expressing

---

[6] Employer-Labour Conference, National Agreement, 1972, clause 3(h).

the agreed view that men should not "introduce claims of benefit to themselves only in order to restore their former relative earning power". Principles were laid down regarding interpretation of equal work, and the processes to be followed in the event of disagreement. There were also provisions regarding anomalies, incentive payment schemes, the interpretation of the term "conditions of employment", provisions of machinery in the event of disputes and an agreement to meet in September 1973 to review the operation of the National Agreements, i.e. both the First and the Second.

The 1972 Agreement was a considerable step forward in central bargaining of a framework agreement. The increasing sophistication of the pay provisions reflect the institutional pressures which emerged during the operation of the First Agreement as well as the changing attitudes of the central representatives of both trade unions and employers. Both sides are beginning to think in national rather than sectional terms, although of course they are still responsive to sectional pressures from their constituents.

Netherlands

The voluntarily-agreed tripartite incomes policy has ended. The trade unions were under increasing pressure from their rank and file members to withdraw from participation in an incomes policy. A major cause of this was the excessively high pressure of demand which meant that the restraint in wage increases required by the formal provisions of incomes policy exceeded the restraints that it was reasonable to expect workers and wage negotiators to exercise. It is probably fair to say that incomes policy was subjected to too great a pressure and insufficient restraint on demand levels. During incomes policy it was a common occurrence for firms to pay black wages, that is payments higher than the standard wages laid down in the income policy provisions. In addition there was some tendency for foremen to act as labour brokers in that they recruited labour to the firm or they were in charge of a group of workers and were prepared to move as a group in response to the payment of black wages. It was increasingly believed that adherence to the provisions of the incomes policy by trade

unions attempting to observe the policy in their formal negotiations was leading to effective discrimination against them.
Accordingly the official trade union movements, in order to
maintain their membership, felt obliged to withdraw from an
incomes policy. In addition they were increasingly dissatisfied
with the general social and economic policies implemented by
the government.

In 1970 the average level of unemployment was 1·3 per cent
which was slightly higher than that for economically comparable
situations in the past. However, the pressure on wages was
rather higher than in the past. This was due in part to the
ending of the formal voluntary incomes policy and also to
increased pressure from below, from the rank and file, for
higher wage increases. Many of the collective wage bargains
for 1970 and 1971 geared wage increases to movements in the
price index. Average earnings for industrial employees in 1970
as provided for in collective agreements were of the order of
9·5 per cent. This would have led to an increase in wages per
unit cost of something over 4 per cent. Increased pressures of
demand in the economy could have been expected to have
pushed wage increases and unit labour cost increases beyond
this point in 1971. The government reacted towards the end of
1970 by implementing restrictive monetary policies, and by
increasing taxation. The government's policies were intended
to tackle the question of inflation from the viewpoint of both
expenditure, i.e. demand, and costs. The linking of wage
increases to movements in the price index, of course, made it
more imperative than on some previous occasions to restrict
the increases in prices no matter what their cause. Towards the
end of 1970 the Cabinet took the view that it should invoke
Article 10 of the Wages and Incomes Act which would allow
it to impose statutory limits on wage increases. This decision
was taken in the context of a package of measures to restrain
the general pressures of demand and increases in costs. In some
ways the wage inflation was aggravated by the existence of
index clauses so that the price increases resulting from the
first stage increase in wages would in themselves provide
grounds for secondary increases in wages as a result of increases
in the price index. The additional stress that this would impose
on the labour market was recognised in the budget memoran-

dum for 1971 but it was thought that the secondary and possibly subsequent increases in wages, labour costs, and prices, resulting from the indexation of wages would create even more adverse situations.

In early 1970 the government adopted the Wages and Incomes Act over the opposition of the various trade union federations. They probably succeeded only because the issue was linked to a vote of confidence. In particular, trade union federations opposed the sections of the Act which enabled the Minister of Social Affairs to interfere in those cases where collectively agreed wage increases might be thought to endanger the economy. The NVV[7] strongly urged in the Social and Economic Council, when this body considered the government's proposals on income, that there had to be more fundamental changes in the ratio of employment incomes and other incomes before they could co-operate. The trade unions did not respond favourably to the government's invitation in July 1970 to take part in discussions with government and employers' associations on the development of the economic situation. In particular they were reluctant to take part in discussions in advance of the report of the special committees of the Social and Economic Council which had been established as a result of trade union pressure to report on wage and price policy. Moreover, the unions took the view that the government would have already determined its basic economic strategy for 1971 and that therefore discussions on incomes policy would be meaningless to trade unionists because they would not be able to influence in any significant way other aspects of social and economic policy.

At the end of August strikes broke out in the Amsterdam and Rotterdam dockyards for higher wages. The basic cause of these was the activities of the *Koppelbazen* (recruiters who seek to induce workers to change their place of employment) who contract workers on a non-permanent basis for enterprises. These temporary contract workers, skilled, semi-skilled and unskilled, received higher pay than the permanently employed workers and this gave rise to the discontent. The trade unions initially supported the strikes and after lengthy negotiations

---

[7] The socialist federation of trade unions.

reached agreement for a wage increase of 25 guilders a week for dockers on condition that further wage negotiations began before the 1st November, 1970. However, by this time an unofficial organisation *Comité Arbeitersnacht* (Committee for Workers' Power) rejected the agreement and demanded a wage increase of 75 guilders a week. The industrial unrest spread to various parts of the country. The officials of the trade unions and employers' associations continued to discuss the problems of *Koppelbazen* and reached agreement which was submitted to the Minister of Social Affairs requesting that this form of recruiting contract workers should be subject to a licence from the Ministry. In addition they agreed that there should be a Ministry approved improvement in income over 1970 up to a gross amount of 400 guilders. The Minister accepted the recommendation on licensing recruitment of contract workers and the unions successfully negotiated a lump sum payment of 400 guilders in many cases. In some industries this was to be paid in monthly instalments. In some large firms, e.g. Philips, Unilever, Shell and AKZO (Chemicals) agreement was reached only after strike action had taken place. By the beginning of November 1970 agreements had been made so that two million out of three million employed had received or were due to receive a lump sum payment of 400 florins.

The anti-inflationary measures taken by government were regarded by the trade unions and by the Social and Economic Council as endangering the possibility of voluntary agreement between the social partners so that voluntary action to restrain inflation was regarded as much less likely. In October 1970 the Social and Economic Council declared itself unanimously in favour of not applying the restrictive clauses of the Wages and Incomes Act. The government, after failing to reach agreement between the employers and trade unions on mutually accept- able policy measures announced that wages which were due to be renewed under existing contracts on either 1st January or 1st April, 1971 could be increased only by 3 per cent and by a further 2 per cent three months from the initial date. Res- triction was to apply until the 1st July, 1971. The lump sum demand of 400 guilders could not be included in the wage increases for 1971 even though they had been agreed. Union movements opposed this measure and called a one-hour stop-

page of work on 15th December to coincide with the discussion
of the measures in the capital's Second Chamber. The Second
Chamber of Parliament revised the government's proposals so
that the lump sum of 400 guilders could be included and the
wage increases for contracts terminating on 1st January or
1st April, 1971 were to be 3 per cent immediately with a
further 1 per cent three months later. The three trade union
federations meeting in their central consultative body decided
to advise their members to seek an improvement in disposable
income in real terms for 1971 which would be a little below the
increase in productivity. They also recognised that the measures
of the government could not be overturned. It thus appears
that particularly large wage increases will be sought after
1st July, 1971.

The government's attempts to impose a form of wage
restraint on a unilateral basis, consequent upon failure to reach
tripartite agreement can therefore be seen as at best a short-
term measure. In this respect it seems to follow the usual
reaction to temporary severe legislative restraint in that after
the restraining period is over the unions seek particularly large
wage increases. The policy to reach a voluntary policy on
tripartite lines can be seen as stemming from two main causes.
Firstly the inability to secure agreement on general economic
policies so that unions regard government-favoured wage
policies as unduly restrictive on workers, and secondly the
unwillingness of rank and file trade unionists to accept what
they regard as unduly severe wage restraint, which means that
the trade union movement in order to preserve its membership
is unable to agree to limit increases in money too far below the
level of expectations of their members.

CHAPTER 2

Industrial Relations Aspects of Incomes Policies

It is accepted for present purposes that ordinary demand management policies are insufficiently effective so that some form of prices and incomes policy is regarded as desirable. The case for or against an incomes policy will not therefore be considered. The orthodox economic analysis of a prices and incomes policy have not been considered in any detail, although on occasions they will necessarily intrude on the discussion of industrial relations.

It is not suggested that all the points made will apply to every incomes policy in every country. There are a number of different forms of incomes policy and general statements can only hope to be applicable to some of them. It is assumed, however, that the policy is essentially a voluntary one, although there may be some sanctions, and that it is more than a short-term emergency measure. It is not possible to say exactly what the industrial relations effects will be. They will be influenced by the type of policy, the traditions, methods and institutions of industrial relations in the country concerned as well as the basic acceptance of the objectives of the policy by the two social partners and government. The following pages will therefore indicate areas where problems may arise rather than attempt to say exactly how they will arise and what form the problems will take. The discussion will concentrate on the problems that may arise in regard to trade unions. This is not to imply that only employment incomes should be covered by incomes policy; the term is taken in fact to refer to a prices and incomes policy and most, if not all incomes, are assumed to be affected. Many of the problems raised by reference to wages and trade unions will have a direct counterpart in employers' associations ensuring that their members do not break the incomes side of the policy, either by granting wage increases in excess of the policy requirements or in respect of other forms of incomes. There will be similar problems in ensuring that the central organisations of employers can effectively commit their members to the price conditions of the policy.

The basic objective of a voluntary prices and incomes policy is to induce those responsible for price and income decisions to take decisions different from those that they would have taken in the absence of the policy. It may be believed that this is not possible, either in principle, in which case there is no point in further discussion of a voluntary prices and incomes policy, or in practice, in which case it is necessary to consider the reasons why this aim may be unattainable in particular circumstances at specific times. Alternatively it may be argued that it is not possible in certain conditions to induce changes in behaviour sufficient to ensure the complete absence of inflation; it might be that a more modest and realistic target should therefore be set. This would not alter the basic purpose of a prices and incomes policy as here defined. It might be added that a great deal of collective bargaining already requires some individuals to accept decisions different from those they would have taken in the absence of the collective bargaining arrangements and procedures as actually practised. For example, an agreement might cover a number of different grades in a plant and it is quite possible that some of those grades, and certainly some of the individuals, might have received higher increases if the bargain had been conducted on a more fragmented basis. This is in fact one of the problems that may arise in an incomes policy, that the degree of pressure resulting from tendencies towards centralisation of decision-taking can become intolerable. But even within what is often regarded as a decentralised bargaining system there is some tendency towards inducing different decisions in respect of some individuals or groups by the very act of bargaining collectively.

Starting from the premise that the general economic conditions—pressure of demand, interest rate, types of taxes, etc.—would lead to a certain rate of change of prices and incomes, the objective of incomes policy therefore is to obtain a lower rate of increase in incomes and thus prices, or to obtain a higher rate of increase in productivity for a given increase in incomes so obtaining a lower rate of increase in prices, or to obtain a lower rate of increase in prices by securing a lower rate of increase in profits. This might be regarded as equivalent to attempting to lower a Phillips curve, but this could ignore the second of the possible objectives, that of increasing productivity growth for any given rate of change of employment income. It does not necessarily follow therefore that an incomes policy will concentrate on holding down the rate of growth of money wages; it might prefer to influence prices through productivity changes and accept that money wages will rise to the same extent as they would without a policy. In this case the objective of the policy is to induce the parties to collective bargaining, or those responsible for actions which can increase productivity, to take a different decision, one which will lead to faster productivity growth.

Most incomes policies seek to induce those responsible for determining employment incomes to settle for smaller increases in money terms, which, if the package of economic policies implemented by the government is successful, should nevertheless mean at least equal and possibly larger increases in real incomes than would be the case without a policy. The relationship and distinction between real and money income is crucial to the attempts to persuade the bargainers to take different decisions. It is also the weak point in the chain of events in that it provides the greatest source of potential difficulty for the continuation of the policy.

If trade unions are to settle for a smaller money increase than they could otherwise obtain, it is necessary to convince them that it is to their advantage to do so; appeals and exhortations based on general statements about the national interest are not sufficient. One assertion can be made with some certainty—no individual trade union can be expected to accept a lower increase in money terms than it knows it can get in isolation, i.e., a union will refuse unless it believes that a number, if not all of the other trade unions, will exercise some similar restraint. It is a necessary condition therefore that the general agreement of the trade union movement be obtained if a voluntary incomes policy is to stand any chance of success, and this may require assurances that other forms of income will be subject to policy pressures.

Centralisation of Trade Union Organisation

Trade unions compete between themselves to some extent either for members or for prestige. In addition, there may be political or ideological differences between trade unions or their leaders which make a unified approach to incomes policy difficult. For the moment it will be assumed that no such complications exist. The importance of ensuring that the restraint exercised by an individual union does not impinge discriminatingly on its members will create a tendency within the trade union movement for a greater degree of centralisation in wage claims. In the absence of an incomes policy normal collective bargaining over wage matters can be centralised, e.g. Sweden, or decentralised, e.g. the United Kingdom and the United States. Incomes policy gives an impetus to centralisation for a number of reasons.

Firstly, as already suggested, trade unions will wish to ensure that other unions follow the policy restraints and this is easiest done if there is a general central wage settlement. Secondly, it is probable that if the system is a decentralised one, the government will wish to create some machinery for the application of the policy. For example, in Britain the vetting of proposed wage settlements was done by the appropriate government department, DEP, Ministry of Power or other sponsoring department. As unions seek to minimise the direct intervention of government in collective bargaining, they will tend to try and take over the vetting duties themselves, and this can be done only by some central trade union authority. It may be that some central authority within the trade union organisation will develop to vet wage claims without there necessarily being centralised co-ordination of claims of centralised bargaining.

Thirdly, incomes policies are not produced or accepted in an economic vacuum. Unions will wish to be consulted about other aspects of economic policies and if they are to exert influence on government in these areas, it is necessary that they present a united front and a coherent front. This will lead to a greater degree of involvement in economic issues, which will tend to strengthen the pressures towards centralisation of wage bargaining. Their own bargaining position *vis-à-vis* government will obviously be reduced if they are unable to offer any changes in their own behaviour in return for changes in social or economic policy, and in order to ensure that they can deliver some of their bargains they will need to be in a position where they can exert some central influence or control over individual unions. Even if the incomes policy is a weak general approach based on guidelines unions will wish to put forward views on its content, and this requires some degree of centralisation, albeit only to a limited extent. The more seriously the policy is accepted and its terms observed, the stronger these tendencies will become.

The increasing centralisation of trade union organisation need not lead to centralised wage bargaining. If it does not, and if the incomes policy collapses for any reason, there is a danger that the greater degree of centralisation in general policy matters will lead to a higher rate of inflation than otherwise. If unions become used to the practice of central discussion of economic issues and introduce some degree of mutually-agreed tactics into their behaviour, it may be that they will use their strongest individual sectors or branch to set the pace in wage bargaining and then use co-ordinated indus-trial strength to spread the high wage settlements to other industries. Indeed in some situations this approach will be easier to adopt than will centralised wage bargaining, for it allows each individual union to retain its autonomy if it so wishes and provides a temporary coalition of those unions who wish to join together to utilise their relative strengths to the greatest advantage. If any individual union believes it can do better by acting alone, it would be free to do so.

However, the general conclusion is that a voluntary incomes policy will necessarily create tendencies towards a greater degree of centralisation in the trade union movement. Central organisations of unions and employers are involved in dis-cussions and consultations with governments over a wide range of economic and social policy issues. This involvement inevitably impresses upon them the fact that their "bargaining" position with government is weakened if they are unable to commit the individual members to some sort of general economic behaviour. Thus, even if there is no attempt to establish an incomes policy, the central trade union organisation will nevertheless seek to attract to itself greater powers to commit the trade unions to certain lines of action.

Problems Arising from Centralisation

Centralised wage bargaining contains dangers for a trade union movement. If bargaining is decentralised, it is not necessary for the various trade unions to agree on the general range of wage differentials either between occupations or between industries. If any particular group is discontented with the outcome of the various settlements (its own and other unions'), it can seek to change things by its own individual actions in its next bargain. Thus, for example, if any particular occupation feels that it has lost a traditional differential over some other occupation, it can unilaterally seek to restore the original position. Similarly an occupation can seek to alter a traditional differential.

There are two major types of differentials: internal, those that relate to groups covered by the same negotiating machinery, and external, those that relate to groups covered by different negotiating groups.[1] In practice, this distinction may not be so clear-cut. For example, an industry-wide agreement may lay down certain wage differentials for specific occupations, but individual plants within that industry may establish different differentials, either as a result of formal plant bargaining covering all the occupations in the plant or as a result of a series of *ad hoc* fragmented bargains between different groups at different times, including the effects of piece-work and other forms of wage drift. In principle, internal differentials are capable of control by the bargaining parties while external differentials are not. However, if plant bargaining is fragmented, then there may be a number of sets of internal differentials existing within an individual plant. Each set can be controlled by those covered by them, but there is no body which is determining all the differentials within the plant. Moreover, the coverage of any set of fragmented bargaining areas may change through time. Using this terminology we can draw a

---

[1] This distinction is not what is often meant by internal and external differentials, but it is the most useful one for present purposes.

very important distinction. Internal differentials ought to be accepted by all the parties concerned as they have been mutually agreed; external differentials may give rise to a series of leap-frogging claims and counter-claims as different groups seek to change or restore some differential in relation to some other group.

The processes of leap-frogging may be inflationary. However, for trade unions there is one advantage—an individual union does not have to formally agree to a differential *vis-à-vis* other unions. If a union is losing its relative wage position, perhaps as a result of technological change or changing economic conditions, so long as it is operating a system of fragmented bargaining with relatively few internal differentials to maintain, it can continue to advocate a policy of restoring previous relative wages. This advocacy may be crucial from a viewpoint of recruitment and retention of members, and trade unions are well aware that one of their prime tasks is to maintain membership. If there is a broad-based negotiating machinery covering the occupations with whom relativities are changing, it may be necessary for the union to formally agree to a worsening of its relative wages. This is much more difficult for it to do.

Centralised bargaining therefore requires that unions are able to agree on a generally acceptable policy of differentials. With complete centralised bargaining all differentials would be internal, as all occupations and groups would be covered by the same set of negotiations. However, even if this were formally established, it is almost certain that wage drift would occur somewhere, so that some differentials would be altered in practice, and thus the question of effective relative wages would have to be raised in the central negotiations. Evidence of this can be found in the Swedish centralised bargaining system, which now formally incorporates anticipatory action to give higher increases to those sectors where no wage drift will take place. The same issues are being raised in Finland.

Differences of opinion will almost certainly arise between different unions covering different occupations or different sectors. In general terms there will be a conflict over the distribution of income between wage and salary earners. In addition, those representing the lower-paid workers will seek to obtain preferentially large increases, or at least to obtain uniform flat-rate increases which narrow percentage differentials. This is not to suggest that trade unions will make no attempts to redistribute wage income: experience shows that on occasions they do, but it is difficult to obtain general agreement to such redistribution.

Opposition comes from two main sources—from trade union leaders who do not accept a narrowing of differentials and from rank and file members who may reject any narrowing that has been agreed by their officials. Inter-union disagreements can give rise to the first. The second is a general problem and one which increases in importance during an incomes policy. Unions are often criticised for their inability to ensure that rank and file members will always accept and implement agreements made on their behalf. While there may be good reasons for this criticism on occasions, it is also the case that an incomes policy places a greater strain on the relations between leadership and rank and file, and that a point can come where the strain proves intolerable. In free societies trade unions must pay attention to the views and wishes of their members even though these may be contrary to the government's economic policy, and even though the national trade union leadership may wish to follow some alternative course of action. Centralised bargaining in an incomes policy emphasises two great sources of stress between leadership and rank and file, the restraint in money wages and the altering of differentials, and the existence of the second emphasises the irksome nature of the first.

The evidence about the scope for reducing differentials in specific plants or industries as a deliberate act of policy accepted by all the negotiating parties concerned is slight as there have been relatively few such attempts. It might be reasonable to assume that on the whole the rank and file who will be "adversely" affected are more reluctant than trade union leadership to see a narrowing of differentials. One of the paradoxes is that trade unions when they discuss wage differentials centrally, almost inevitably conclude that special help should be given to the lower-paid and yet the best way of actually doing this with collective bargaining is a centralised system with differential increases, something which produces considerable stresses and strains. It is necessary to secure the effective agreement of other trade unions as well as the actual acceptance of the results by their rank and file members. The very act of centralised settlements gives rise to public knowledge of the outcome of the settlement which may well stimulate the rejection of the settlement. If it were possible to give preferential increases to the lower-paid without centralised settlements, it might be possible to secure some effective acceptance of the results. Decentralised bargaining almost by definition cannot help them. They are unable on their own to exercise enough bargaining power to obtain high increases. This is one of the attractions of incomes policies to trade unions. It offers a way of meeting one of their basic objectives of a more equitable distribution of income. Yet to achieve this end, they must become involved in the additional problems of securing general agreement on differentials involved in centralised bargaining.

It is possible to reduce some of the tensions of centralised bargaining by adopting a more flexible system. The central agreement can determine the amount to be given in wage increases in the industry and leave it to the employers and the various trade unions in the industry to allocate the sum. This passes the problems of differentials downwards to the industry, but the repercussions may affect other industries. For example, if industry A gives particularly large increases to a particular occupation that is also employed elsewhere, industry B may feel obliged to give equally large increases in order to retain its labour.

To summarise, it is believed that there will inevitably be tendencies towards increasing the degree of centralisation in trade union policy—formulation in respect of general economic and social policy as a result of an incomes policy. In order to grasp the opportunities to exert influence on government's general policy as part of the bargaining situation that will arise in the course of discussing and seeking to establish an incomes policy, unions will need to obtain some degree of centralisation or the opportunities will not be fully exploited. This may or may not lead to increased centralisation in wage determination. The particular type of policy adopted will, of course, itself influence the strength of the forces towards centralisation; a relatively weak policy that sought to influence expectations through forecasting and indicative planning rather than to express norms and permissible rates of increase with exceptional clauses would exert less pressures towards centralisation. The views in the previous paragraphs are influenced to some extent by the writer's opinion that a stronger form of incomes policy is desirable. If this is not accepted, then the importance placed on centralised bargaining as a desirable, or even perhaps a necessary condition for the long-run success of an incomes policy is somewhat reduced. Nevertheless it is still believed that decentralised bargaining not within a framework of generally acceptable differentials increases the general level of inflationary pressures.

Extent of Commitment to a Voluntary Policy

Trade unions are voluntary organisations. Membership is voluntary in most cases and unions need to rely on the voluntary acceptance of their policies by their members. They have some sanctions, but in the large majority of cases these are not particularly effective, as members can leave the union and avoid the sanction. In those cases where trade union membership is a condition of employment, unions are understandably reluctant to discipline members by expulsion, and in any case there are often legal limitations surrounding the exercise of disciplinary powers by trade unions. In some cases public opinion is ambiguous on this subject. There is often a demand that unions enforce discipline on their members to ensure that certain agreements are kept, in this case wage bargains that are in accord with the incomes policy; yet on other occasions if trade unions discipline their members for breaking other union rules which receive less support from the general public, e.g. group limitations on bonus earnings or seniority and promotion rules, they are likely to be castigated by public opinion and accused of exercising dictatorial powers over the freedom of individuals. Unions are suspicious of the intervention of public opinion, which always seems to them to be anti-union.

The voluntary nature of trade union membership means that individuals must believe that membership is in their immediate interest. If they do not believe this, they will leave. Unions have to retain their membership to survive, and they will not for long deliberately pursue policies which are so unpopular that membership declines. There is a danger that incomes policy with its heavy emphasis on wage restraint is seen as removing the need for, or advantages from, trade union membership. Trade unions cannot take the risk of appearing to be superfluous. To the extent that their membership appreciate the full economic problems and understand that their interests could well be better served by incomes policy and appropriate economic policies, this risk will be reduced; but such appreciation requires a considerable degree of sophistication in economic analysis, a degree, for example, that is not yet found in other sections of the community.

The importance of trade unions being able to commit their members to the restraint aspect of the policy cannot be overstressed. It is the single most important aspect of an incomes policy. The very real difficulties encountered by trade union organisations in persuading their members to accept a policy are often overlooked or under-emphasised by other groups. One important conclusion for industrial relations is that incomes policy will be better served by strong trade unions than by weak ones. Weak unions cannot hope to commit their members with any degree of assurance and, moreover, their membership is likely to be small. Strong unions on the other hand are better placed to commit a large and significant section of the labour force, but, by their strength, can also cause greater damage to a policy if they decide to oppose it. This is a risk that has to be faced. The voluntary acceptance of a policy cannot be guaranteed by any organisation or representatives; it must come from the full rank and file membership and from all the individual companies and plant managers having the authority to change wages or prices. Strong organisation offers a greater possibility of commitment but also carries a greater danger if the commitment turns into opposition. Similarly, decentralised companies with weak central authority cannot commit their managers to observe the policy.

Employers' associations, too, must retain their members; and although it might at first sight appear that a policy of wage restraint will receive wide support from employers so that there will be far fewer internal stresses with employers' organisations, this is not necessarily so. Many individual firms are not averse to increasing wages in tight labour markets, particularly if they believe other employers will not. Indeed, there may be more to gain from increasing wages if others cannot. The greater stresses, however, are likely to come on the non-wage side, from the prices or profits policies. Individual firms may see less benefit in membership of an employers' or commercial association that has committed them to a policy which prevents them increasing prices, and far worse, of actually decreasing them in some situations.

It is necessary therefore for the two sides of industry and the government to recognise the limits beyond which the other parties cannot be pushed. While these limits may be regarded as burdensome by the other parties, failure to appreciate their limiting nature will rob policy discussions of their basis of realism and prevent an effective policy from emerging. Policies which require a degree of commitment of membership by either social partner, which cannot reasonably be expected, will fail and no doubt deserve to do so. Similarly, if the social partners lay down conditions for their participation which they cannot reasonably expect government to meet, they must expect to be disappointed. No government for example can really expect to provide constantly full employment and absolutely steady growth. The techniques of demand management are as yet incapable of providing this even if reinforced with other policies. Unions and employers ought not, therefore, to expect that these conditions can be provided, but if they do, and tell their members that these are the conditions on which participation in the incomes policy is advocated and endorsed, they must expect disillusionment to set in sooner or later. The goals set by, and demanded of, the various parties, must be sufficiently modest and realistic as to be attainable. Similarly, when extolling the virtues of an incomes policy, the expected results must not be overstated or the credibility gap will work against the acceptance of the obligations of the policy.

Inflation or Incomes Policy: the Real Choice?

The most common objective of incomes policy, or the most often used argument to justify workers' co-operation, is the ending of inflation. It may well be that this is not in fact the most sought-after objective of trade unions. The ending of stop-go growth and employment policies might be more attractive to them, and although the stopping of inflation might be a first step in the ending of stop-go, emphasis on the final objective of economic growth with stability might prove to be much more attractive. Also, it is now perhaps the case that governments ought not to advocate as their policy goal absolute price stability and the ending of all inflation. This may well not be a practical proposition. Some degree of inflation might be inevitable. The more realistic, as well as desirable, aim might be to ensure that the rate of inflation does not exceed that of foreign countries. However, if this is achieved in a situation where the absolute rates of inflation escalate so that, say, countries are inflating at twenty or thirty per cent a year, then although any individual country may avoid its balance-of-payments problems by not exceeding the international rate, there may still be objections to the rate of inflation in that it could jeopardise the whole basis of democracy on which the systems rest. But in these circumstances, there is little that any one country can do to avoid this degree of inflation; it becomes an international problem requiring international co-ordinated action. This brief statement, along with much of the discussion of the need for prices and incomes policies for reasons connected with adverse balance of payments situations accepts (implicitly) the view that exchange rates should be fixed. It is of course possible to advocate floating or movable exchange rates in which case the argument alters.

If governments accept a "realistic" view that some degree of inflation is inevitable (at least given our exchange rate policies, commitments to high employment and inflation in other countries), the question arises whether it will have more hope of success for its incomes policy if it starts from a public recognition that some inflation will occur, or whether it should base its policy pronouncements on the objective of price stability. Price stability is a clear objective. It also provides certain macro-level policy guidelines about the permitted rate of changes of certain aggregate variables. On the other hand, most people recognise that it is unrealistic; and therefore, if it stretches credulity too far, it prevents the creation of the goodwill which a voluntary policy needs. Also, complete price stability might require a degree of wage restraint that is so far removed from the expectations of trade unions or their members that it would not be possible to obtain their compliance with the policy requirements. For example, if the price stability requirements permitted a 3 per cent increase in wages but the general expectations of trade unions and their members were, say, 7 per cent, and the employers were willing, or expected, to pay, say, 6 per cent, it might be expecting too much to hope for the 3 per cent settlement. The danger then would be that, because the policy goal was considered ridiculously low, the whole policy became abandoned. A realistic policy might adopt a goal of wage increases of, say, 5 per cent, which might be attainable.

There are problems with the realistic approach, however. Norms or guidelines based on absolute stability leave relatively little room for argument about the size of the increase in aggregate wages; in fact the only scope for discussion is over the question of redistribution of income between aggregate income groups. It becomes possible, once the basic decisions have been taken, to reject any particular wage claim on the grounds that it would endanger the price stability objective. If, however, the policy clearly accepts—indeed aims for—a rate of inflation of, say, 2 per cent, it is possibly more difficult to argue against a particular wage claim that seeks to exceed the agreed level. An individual union can argue that the overall effect of its claim for, say, 8 per cent would be, say, only one-third of one per cent on the general price index; and as inflation of 2 per cent had been accepted, 2·3 would not be a major catastrophe. There might be the danger, therefore, that each wage claim would become a bargaining process between government and the unions concerned about tolerable degree of inflation. However it may be that this is an over-sophisticated point in that a zero-inflation norm would also be subject to pressure as a union argued that 0·3 per cent inflation would be tolerable. What is perhaps the most important point is that there should be discussions between the parties and government as to the level of norm to be set (assuming the policy is based on a norm). In the UK the 1964 policy was not preceded by public discussion and debate about the size of the norm—neither as to what was a desirable norm nor what was an attainable norm; although earlier the National Incomes Commission had accepted the view that a norm should be realistic rather than "pure".

It may be that the concept of an incomes policy based on a "norm" is rejected in favour of a more flexible approach. A too rigid norm would be subject to pressures from price movement abroad (see the Edgren, Faxen and Odhner model for Sweden). Also if the level of money demand fluctuates, either absolutely or in relation to the increase consistent with the maintenance of the "permitted" increase in real consumption under the policy, additional pressures will be exerted which may make it increasingly difficult to hold increases in money terms to the limits set by the norm. This could lead to one of two types of conclusion. Firstly it could be decided to abandon the norm and seek to provide general guide-lines in terms of ranges of increase. Secondly, it could be decided to keep the general approach of a norm but to change its basis from time to time (say year to year). In this way a period of a strict or non-inflationary norm could be followed by a period of a more "realistic" norm which sought to moderate rather than prevent inflation. In this way the tensions created by one period could be allowed to ease somewhat and the relatively less successful results of the following period could themselves be offset by a more rigorous approach in the third period. This would permit a greater degree of flexibility in approach, which although perhaps less successful in particular periods, might allow greater long-run benefits to be obtained as the stresses which would otherwise lead to the break-up of the policy could be contained to some extent thus permitting the policy to be continued. The problem would then arise of how the norm was to be determined from period to period. Trade unions would be suspicious of changes in the basis of calculating the norm, particularly if these appeared to be working against increases in money wage increases. The American experience of changing the basis for calculating the "norm" under the guidelines illustrates this point. The question might then become whether it is easier to obtain agreement to change the basis or whether it is easier to reach agreement on a more or less once-for-all basis whereby the norm once determined in amount or in principle operates for a number of years.

Application of the Policy

According to the type of incomes policy, it might be necessary for some government department or agency to be given responsibility for its implementation. This might involve the vetting of proposed wage increases or price changes. Problems may arise if this task is given to the Ministry of Labour or equivalent department which has a traditional role of conciliation. The traditional role of working towards a settlement acceptable to both sides has often led Departments of Labour to emphasise their independent position. They may have slowly built up a fund of goodwill with both social partners which may disappear if they are now to determine their attitude to industrial disputes not according to their traditional role of peacekeepers, but as policemen applying an incomes policy.

If the Labour Department believe that incomes policy is a short-term operation, they may prefer to protect their long-term position by maintaining good relations with the bargaining partners at the expense of the current requirements of incomes policy. If they do not, but instead apply the policy fairly rigorously, there is a danger that the independent position of the ministry will be jeopardised so that it could be extremely difficult to return to the traditional functions of conciliation and mediation.

In an attempt to avoid this problem, some other government department may be given responsibility for applying the policy. A different problem might then arise. If a strike is threatened over a wage claim, it is possible that the department applying the policy might take a tough line and refuse to approve a settlement which exceeds the policy guide-lines, while the Department of Labour in its peace-keeping role may feel obliged to try and get a settlement even though the terms are out of line with the policy. The same difficulties may arise on the prices side if the departments responsible for vetting price increases or seeking price reductions are the departments traditionally responsible for dealing with the industries concerned. Departments may develop a protective attitude towards "their" industries. They may have created working relationships which they do not wish to see threatened by their own enforced participation as price-policy policemen. If some other department is given the job, there may be conflicts between different government departments.

Government departments are not blindly obedient bodies following the orders of a single source of authority. They have policies and interests, and in some ways corporate personalities, of their own. Conflict of interest or differences of emphasis in the application or interpretation of policies between different departments is not, therefore, unusual. The mere existence of a prices and incomes policy will not change this and indeed might sharpen the differences by raising new and important areas of conflict. This can affect industrial relations by changing the attitude towards and relations with the Department of Labour and unions.

Intervention in Bargaining

A voluntary policy requires that wage settlements conform to the policy outlines. In an ideal situation where all parties fully accepted the obligations imposed by a policy, the only requirement would be to make sure that it was possible for all negotiators to know what the policy required of them. For example, with a guideposts policy with exception clauses, the exception clauses must be capable of application to specific circumstances without undue difficulty. They should be sufficiently clear so that those who genuinely want to observe the policy are able to do so. This requirement of clarity in detail conflicts with the task of seeking agreement from the social partners on the policy terms. Agreement is more likely to be reached on general principles, and the more that details are discussed the more difficulties will arise. If they are not discussed, however, they may simply be postponed, and the disagreements emerge when the general conditions are being applied to specific cases. Such areas as differentials, desirable distribution of manpower, structural changes in employment, preferential increases for the lower-paid, may have to receive special treatment if the unions are to co-operate, but the unions themselves may be unable to agree on the specific details, and there may be very little agreement between them and the employers. While this suggests, perhaps, that the policy is doomed to failure, it is not necessarily so. The benefits of the policies once established may be appreciated so that attitudes subsequently change and some level of agreement becomes possible, although it would not have been earlier. Both parties would be hesitant to commit themselves too firmly to details until they have some experience of the actual working of the policy.

However, in addition to raising problems of securing agreement the provisions of explicit details of the nature of exception clauses increases the complexity of incomes policy. In particular, as the exception clauses are made more explicit, they tend to multiply. The greater the number of exceptional circumstances, the more difficult it may be to secure adherence to the policy as more and more firms or groups of workers believe that they genuinely qualify under one or other exception clause. There is some conflict between the desire to obtain justice or secure some other economic goal, and the need to keep the number of exceptional clauses within limits. The less explicit the exception clauses, the greater the need for some agency external to the bargaining parties to interpret the provisions for them or to check whether a particular bargain does indeed really qualify for exceptional treatment.

However, even though there may be fairly detailed statements of the policy, there will probably be occasions when a settlement is, or looks like being, contrary to the policy. Knowledge of what is required may be a necessary, but is not a sufficient condition for success. Even with a highly centralised bargaining system with no exception clauses, the settlement might exceed the desired level. The question then arises of the stage at which government, or its agency, should seek to intervene and obtain a settlement more in line with the policy.

If intervention is left until after the parties have reached agreement, it will be more difficult for the government to change it. Once the parties have reached an agreement, there are a number of pressures on them to adhere to it; it is, after all, *their* settlement which they have jointly reached and for which they accept joint responsibility. If on the other hand government tries to intervene at an earlier stage to ensure that the settlement does not conflict with the policy, there is a danger that both parties will object. They may claim that a voluntary system should leave the parties free to arrive at settlements in line with policy requirements as best they can and government intervention at an early stage might be seen as undue interference with free collective bargaining. If this is seen as an attack on a basic principle it might be regarded as a more serious threat than the economic difficulties which are held to justify the policy so that the parties conclude that their long-term interests would be better served by withdrawing co-operation with the policy.

It is of course true that if the two parties really accept the policy, government intervention will be minimal, but realism requires some anticipatory provisions. It is very unlikely that all decisions will conform to the policy. Even if formally bargained wage increases do, there will undoubtedly be wage drift in some sectors. Thus even though it is not suggested that every decision must conform strictly to the last letter of the policy, there will almost certainly be cases where the government will wish to intervene to influence more directly the outcome of particular negotiations or to seek to change a decision already taken. The latter action might involve changing some other feature of the settlement and not the wage increase itself. The National Board for Prices and Incomes, in the United Kingdom, endorsed some wage increases which were in themselves in excess of the policy, but made them acceptable by obtaining or recommending changes in working practices which, by increasing productivity, made the increases permissible under the productivity exception clause of the then operative policy.

Collusion

Collective bargaining requires that the parties accept joint and collective responsibility for their settlements once they have been agreed. It has been suggested above that this can create problems for an incomes policy if the agreement made provides increases in excess of the amounts permissible under the policy. The joint approach of unions and employers may develop even further.

With some sorts of income policy there may be a tendency towards collusion between trade unions and employers to further their joint interests at the expense of the community or the policy-makers. For example, under a guidelines policy both sides may wish to qualify for an exceptionally high increase on the grounds, say, of distribution of labour. The employers might take the view that their position in the tight labour market would be eased if they could give an above-the-norm increase. It might well be that the two parties would also press for a price increase in order to justify the extra wage increase. In the extreme cases, employers may be willing to grant a particular wage increase providing it can be covered by higher prices which the government may not be willing to permit. A strike may take place because the union is determined to obtain a wage increase. Both parties will press the government to permit a price increase. In this situation the strike is as much against the government's price policy as against the employers' refusal to grant a wage increase immediately and unconditionally. The rest of the trade union movement may then be faced by a dilemma when deciding whether to support the strike or not.

The development of joint interests by the two social partners might be regarded as a desirable growth of mutual interest and appreciation of each others' problems and difficulties. On the other hand, it might be thought that this joint interest is harmful to the general good in that the two parties are combining to take advantage of other sections of the community. Collusive action which expresses itself in higher prices may result in a redistribution of income between sectors rather than between factors. The attempts by other sectors to restore previous relative incomes can be no less inflationary. Improvements in some aspects of industrial relations at branch or sector level are not necessarily to be welcome; it depends on the economic effects of such improvements.

Arbitration

In some countries it is the practice to submit wage claims to arbitration if the two parties are unable to agree a settlement. The first question to arise is whether arbitrators should be influenced by the existence and terms of an incomes policy when reaching their decision. There is little, if any, agreement on the criteria normally to be adopted by arbitrators in arriving at their decisions in disputes of interests, but there is often a belief that arbitrators are independent in that they are not subject to instruction by any outside body and will arrive at their decision in their own way after taking into account the arguments of both parties. There is often a feeling that arbitrators in some way provide "justice" and arrive at their decisions according to the merits of the arguments. More cynical approaches may suggest that arbitrators split the difference between the two sides or alternatively, always give the lion's share to the lion, thereby approximating to the result that would have been reached by the two parties had they been able to agree themselves and not therefore gone to arbitration.

If arbitrators are required to observe the conditions of an incomes policy, there may be reluctance to go to arbitration if it is thought that a more generous interpretation of the policy, or improved chances of evading the more rigorous conditions, may exist in ordinary collective bargaining. There may develop the feeling that arbitrators will stick closer to the restraint provisions of the policy than would negotiators and therefore arbitration will fall into disrepute. Alternatively, arbitrators may refuse to be bound or guided by the policy and hand down the same decisions as they would have given without a policy. In this case there will be either an increase in the number of cases going to arbitration, or the government or body responsible for applying the incomes policy will, on the grounds of equity, intercede to prevent the arbitration awards from being applied. The awards would in this case be reduced to match those reached by negotiators who are observing the policy. This interference with the results of arbitration can arouse deep resentment among trade unions even though it may be accepted that the awards break the policy conditions. The principle of the sanctity of arbitration awards is one which might be defended even though the details of specific cases might not be supported. There is something inherently contradictory in the eyes of trade unionists in external interference with the outcome of arbitration. There is equally something contradictory in the reluctance of trade unions to concede that arbitrators should be bound by the conditions of an incomes policy if that policy is in principle accepted by them and being observed in voluntary wage negotiations.

One explanation is that unions believe that incomes policy will be only a short-term phenomenon which will be imposed to meet emergency situations and relaxed when economic conditions improve. Arbitration is seen as having long-term benefits, and therefore they are reluctant to sacrifice the independent basis of arbitration on the altar of short-term expediency, particularly an expediency the need for which they may not yet have fully accepted. By the same argument, incomes policy might impose long-term damage on an industrial relations system if, in order to achieve short-term improvements, it undermines or destroys the accepted independence and impartiality of arbitration. This could be particularly unfortunate in some countries, e.g. the United Kingdom, where arbitration has been slowly established in some industries as the preferred way of settling major disputes peacefully.

If the arbitrators are allowed to give awards which clearly conflict with incomes policy as interpreted by the appropriate body for applying policy, the existence of double standards will create stresses which might prove too strong for the policy to contain. The same arguments apply in other cases which are similar to arbitration, such as the British Wages Councils where, if the representatives of the two sides of industry cannot agree, the independent members vote for the proposal of one side or the other.[2] They act not as arbitrators but as independents who can choose the proposals of one side in their entirety. (The proposal contained in the Emergency Public Interest Protection Bill as described in President Nixon's statement of 27 February 1970, for the establishment of final offer selection groups is along these lines.)

Comparability

There is strong evidence to support the view that comparability plays an important role in wage claims. Increases and/or levels in other industries, occupations, plants or groups within the same plant are widely used as justification for wage increases. It also seems that to a considerable extent average earnings in

---

[2] Strictly speaking, they vote for or against proposals from each side and so could in principle vote against all proposals. If the two sides agree, the independents have no vote; they participate only when there is disagreement.

different sectors move more or less together. In some cases this is the result of a deliberate policy of solidarity by the unions. In other cases it seems to be the result of a mixture of forces, coercive comparisons, independent decisions which in aggregate produce a degree of uniformity even though the disaggregated individual decisions may not be particularly similar, economic pressure, institutionalised linking of various wage settlements, wage rounds and so on. In other cases comparability is formally established as the basis for determining movements in wages or salaries, particularly in the public sector. In these cases comparability is not only the *criterion* for determining the size of wage increases, it is also the *method* by which wages and salaries are determined.

If the incomes policy is observed fairly strictly, claims based on general comparisons ought not to provide any strong inflationary pressure. Comparability with specific industries or occupations might be undesirable, however, if these have received a preferentially high increase under the policy, e.g. in order to reallocate labour, help the low-paid or reward special contributions to increased productivity. If the special factors are not present in other industries, comparability would not be proper under the policy. One reason why governments seek to limit the application of general comparability is that once some wage increases exceed the norm, comparability would ensure that other wage increases exceed the norm. Excessive increases become self-perpetuating. Similarly, the reason why trade unions are reluctant to abandon all appeal to general comparability is that they do not wish to fall behind the other groups; if increases are to be self-perpetuating, they are not going to be left out of the general coverage. If the government is confident that its policy will be successful, general comparability carries no danger. Under any form of policy which permits certain groups of workers to have preferentially high wage increases in specified conditions, governments must try to ensure that those increases are not received by others as a result of comparability claims.

The belief in the justice of claims based on comparability runs deep in the trade union movement. Appeals to history often appear to be the strongest they can make. Whether these appeals are in fact successful may well be less important than whether they are believed to be. Whenever a basic tenet of belief or action is removed, it is necessary to substitute something else. In this case it would be necessary to provide some other generally accepted principle by which general wage increases could be made. Incomes policy would, by its very nature, seek to impose some principle based on rationality and economic requirements, e.g. differential wage movements to encourage the desired distribution of labour between industries and localities. As we have suggested earlier, this raises two problems. Firstly, the selection of the criteria which are to be substituted, and secondly, the securing of general and formal agreement to the adoption of the new criteria not only in principle but also the acceptance in practice of the actual wage levels and relativities that would in fact result from the application of the criteria. It is likely to prove extremely difficult for trade unions or employers to agree on these amongst themselves, far less collectively.

Where the trade union movement adopts the principle of solidarity, comparability becomes incorporated into the wage system which must become centralised. In this, assuming that there is adequate control of wage drift, or some agreed non-inflationary way of compensating for it if it occurs, comparability provides no undue difficulties as long as the wage drift and compensatory action (comparability) do not exceed the permitted rate of wage increase. Problems perhaps arise most acutely in those incomes policies based on some form of guideposts with a norm and exception clauses for higher increases where they are decentralised wage settlements (e.g. the United Kingdom policy, 1965–70). The policy was applied with varying degrees of rigour and success, so that at certain times some groups received increases which appeared to be higher than they ought to have been. Other groups tried to press claims based on comparability although the general policy outlines condemned such claims. The civil service relied on comparability as the basis of their method of pay determination in a formal institutionalised way using the Pay Research Unit to produce refined comparability with jobs of similar skills and imputs. In this situation, to reject comparability completely as a basic of wage or salary increases would have meant the abandonment of a method of pay

3

determination which had the support of trade unions and government "official" side and would have required the acceptance of a new method of pay determination. This is a much more serious problem than merely changing the *reasons* for which wage increases can be given. To abandon comparability means that some other acceptable basis of wage determination has to be produced. Straight bargaining is unlikely to prove acceptable. Normal bargaining sanctions are absent or there are inhibitions about their use. Arbitration is often rejected as a long-term method; the absence of agreed guidelines by which the arbitrator shall determine his award introduces an undesirable element of uncertainty, and the existence of those guidelines should, in most cases, remove the need for arbitration as the two parties ought to be able to apply them for themselves. Moreover, arbitration might be influenced by the existence of an incomes policy.

It will be necessary for the government to give considerable thought to the role of comparability in an incomes policy. The extent and nature of the problem will depend on the practices and institutions of the country concerned and the type of policy it is trying to introduce. Merely to condemn comparability as an integral part of the inflationary process is insufficient. It is so well-established in the thinking and behaviour of so many trade unions that neither condemnatory statements nor pious expressions of the need for change, no matter how sound the underlying economic analysis, will suffice to obtain its abandonment. For not only does the use of comparability reflect institutional and political factors, it also seems to include economic policy-making, too, for it is widely believed by employers that failure to maintain customary differentials will lead to a loss of labour or inability to recruit additional labour. There is a strong coalition of interests and arguments, therefore, apparently underpinning the use of and justification for comparability. The strength of this as a force in wage determination is exemplified in the Swedish EFO model[3] of inflation where the forces of comparability, reinforced

---

[3] See G. Edgren, K. O. Faxen and C. O. Odhner, "Wages, Growth and the Distribution of Income", *Swedish Journal of Economics*, 1969.

or formalised by the solidarity principle, extend the increases in wages in the competitive sector throughout the economy.

Government Employees

Public employees are often in a particularly invidious position in an incomes policy. Governments believe that they must demonstrate to other employers that they are exercising the required restraint in their own capacity as employers. They therefore often take the lead in observing policy conditions, although in other respects they may tend to follow the developments in employment practices by outside employers. Public employees not unnaturally feel aggrieved by this attitude and see themselves as perpetually victimised by the double role of government as leader of opinion and as employer. Equally, government departments themselves, as opposed to government in the form of political policy-makers, may regret their perpetual position in the vanguard of incomes policy. They are concerned to recruit and retain a satisfactory labour force, and the intervention by "political" government policy may impinge upon what they regard as good employer practice. Thus, both employers and unions in the public sector may find their peculiar position as representatives or indicators of the seriousness of the government's intent, unduly irksome. At the same time, government will be under pressure from other employers, and possibly unions, to demonstrate its conviction in its own policies by applying the terms of incomes policy to its own employees.

The less centralised and formal the incomes policy, the greater the pressure by government on its own employees is likely to be. If there is a single central settlement, government employees will probably feel discriminated against only in respect of wage drift increases received by other sectors, and they will probably find other groups in similar positions in other industries. The question of compensation for non-drift is more likely to be raised in the central settlement and, hopefully, an agreed solution emerge, which, as it has been agreed by other unions and employers, will not lead to complaints by private employers that government is adopting a hypocritical position. On the other hand, where the policy is in a weak form, such as

general exhortation to employers and unions to avoid inflationary wage settlements, government will probably find
itself under the strongest pressure to "set a good example".
This is when public employees' unions will complain that they
are being particularly and unfairly discriminated against.

Collective bargaining in the public sector necessarily differs
from bargaining in the private sector. The added stress that
can arise from an incomes policy can lead to a worsening of
relations between unions and government departments. Where
the departments in their role of employers disagree with the
government policy, there is an obvious danger that unions will
come into direct conflict with government on a political level.
If it is no longer possible for public service unions to exercise
their functions as they see them through bargaining with
departments on something like the same basis as private sector
bargaining, it is to be expected that public service unions will
turn to political expression in order to pursue their aims.

The Nature of Bargaining

It has been suggested that bargaining may change in one way
in that there will be a tendency towards collusion or an em-
phasising of joint interests between unions and employers. Part
of this tendency may express itself in a change in the processes
and techniques of bargaining. One of the aims of incomes
policy is to place wage and salary determination on a more
rational basis in that increases given should conform to some
previously agreed policy. There is a specific rejection of the
approach of leaving wages to the free play of market and
institutional power forces. These may, of course, be taken into
account when determining the general policy outlines and
when deciding which sectors might have additional increases
or what criteria are to be satisfied for extra increases, but once
the policy has been agreed they are expected to play a much
less important role.

Collective bargaining will change its nature. It will no longer
suffice to bargain by the old methods. Increased reliance has to
be placed on statistical or factual arguments intended to
demonstrate that the group concerned do indeed qualify under
one of the exception clauses. Straight power arguments will

have less weight and, in fact, ought to play no overt part once the policy is determined. Trade union leaders will have to adapt to the new conditions and this will impose considerable strains on them and their organisations in some instances. It is not easy to impose a new set of conditions to influence the behaviour of wage bargainers. Established leaders may well be suspicious of statistical arguments and be reluctant to hand over part of the bargaining process to backroom research workers. At the very least, there will be strains inside the organisation. These pressures will, of course, spread downward through the union. Conferences of lay delegates will have to be converted to the new grounds on which wage claims can be based, and there is something contradictory to trade unionists in the argument that pure industrial strength is no longer a sufficient or even acceptable reason for pressing for a wage increase. Industrial strength is one of the major weapons trade unions have, and they have learned over a long period that they must build up their strength. Whether other groups agree with this underlying philosophy is far less important than whether trade unionists do. If they do, the task of education will be more difficult and this means that other groups must have patience. It is futile to expect instant conversions. There are very few St. Pauls in trade unions.

Employers' Profits

Even though unions accept the underlying premises of an incomes policy and persuade their members to accept the necessary restraint, the policy will come under severe pressure from unions if there are sharp increases in profits. The very success of an incomes policy creates its own problems. If economic improvement leads to an increase in profits, quite apart from cyclical movements, trade unions worry about income distribution. Moreover, the increase in profits provides opportunities for opponents of the policy to appear to demonstrate that the restraints are being applied in a discriminatory way. Given the cyclical fluctuations in profits, it is relatively easy to show that profits have increased in relation to some past period or other.

Even with a rigorous price policy, the level of profits will fluctuate and can increase for reasons other than merely increased efficiency. Higher world prices can lead to higher profits even though there is strict price control over all domestic prices and even if the policy is obtaining the price decreases which are so difficult to secure. Some incomes policies permit higher profits if they are the result of increased efficiency in conditions of competition, but it does not in fact follow that unions agree that this is just or accept the resulting redistribution of income. Sharp increases in profits place severe strains on trade unions in an incomes policy. Measures to prevent such increases cannot be entirely successful and so attention should be focused on ways of preventing the existence of these increases in profits from leading to a breakdown of the policy. This might lead to tax schemes to neutralise the profit increases or capital profit-sharing schemes to share the benefits and it will probably have to be accepted that if the policy is to continue for long, unions will wish to influence policy regarding profits.

In the Swedish EFO model of wage movements, with competitive and sheltered sectors, the process is that wages in the competitive sector will rise if world prices of the products rise by more than the negotiated wage increase.[4] If this were not so, and assuming that prices of exports rose to match world prices, with fixed exchange rates, there would be an increase in profits. This would be unacceptable to trade unions.

If prices did not rise, the home industry, both wages and profits, would be subsidising foreign customers by selling for less than market prices. If wages in the competitive sector rise in this way, the sociological, political or institutional forces at work in wage determination, will tend to result in similar sorts of increases being received by workers in the sheltered sector. Thus, put extremely crudely, forces concerned with the distribution of income between wages and profits will ensure that wages rise in line with product prices as determined on world markets, and forces then concerned with the distribution of income between different wage sectors and groups will ensure that the same rate of increase is spread throughout the employed labour force. In these circumstances, it might be argued that an incomes policy which set a norm below the rate of

---

[4] Ibid.

growth of world prices must fail, given fixed exchange rates.

If it were possible to ensure that there was no undue rise in profits, however, the wage increases might be contained. If the competitive sector obtains its wage increase it is still possible that the spread of it to other sectors can be prevented, if there are barriers in the labour market such as differential and discriminatory unemployment among different occupations, or other restrictions caused by race or colour, for example. Otherwise, both the economic forces as understood by employers and trade unions, will be tending towards the same results—similar increases all round.

Wage Drift

Management too has a major responsibility for containing wage drift. It is not possible to allocate responsibility only to trade unions, and urge them to control their members. In many instances, wage drift occurs because there has been a jointly-agreed decision by workers and management. In relatively few cases does wage drift occur as a result of unilateral action by workers or local trade union representatives. In other cases drift occurs without any current joint decision being overtly taken, as when productivity increases with constant piecework prices. This is a situation which brings out the conflict between public and private interest in one of its sharpest forms. To the company, increased productivity accompanied by higher earnings is not a bad thing and may well make a significant reduction in unit costs. The private interests of the company, and of its employees, would lie in encouraging such developments. If, however, such increased earnings lead to claims for corresponding increases by other groups to maintain customary differentials, or on solidarity grounds to total increases of equal percentages in other sectors, public interest would oppose the action. Strictly speaking, public interest should oppose the spreading of the increases to other sectors, but it may not be possible within the policy to prevent this. British productivity bargaining came under criticism on this account during the operation of the Labour Government's incomes policy. No evidence was produced to show that productivity bargained increases spread to other firms, where no compensating increases in productivity were forthcoming; but equally, despite the allegations, there was no substantial evidence to show that they did not spread.

In some countries, wage increases are often given by relatively low levels of management, say first- or second-line supervision. There may be no clearly defined and comprehensive wage policy within the firm. Trade unions complain on occasions that companies adopt an *ad hoc* approach to wages in contrast to their very carefully thought-out policies for marketing or production. Incomes policy requires more thought and attention to wage systems and structures. It also means that employers must accept their joint responsibilities for wage increases.

Government Policies

Governments must realise that the existence of an incomes policy does not mean that they can ease up on their demand management policies to the point of not taking unpopular actions. Although incomes policy is intended to induce decisions different from those that would otherwise have resulted in the same demand conditions, the changes expected should not be too great. Thus demand conditions cannot get too far out of line if some degree of restraint is to be exercised. Governments should co-ordinate various policies, e.g. demand and manpower policies, so that firms losing labour which is needed elsewhere, should not be in a position to increase wages in an attempt to retain it, and labour should be guided to other employment. Demand conditions should not be such that manpower policy is jeopardised.

A more rational, less inflationary, way of tackling manpower and wages problems must consider labour allocation. It may be that there will have to be a greater degree of mobility of labour than they have tended to so far (some trade unionists are now expressing this view). This could lead to more geographical or industrial or occupational mobility which would be induced by non-wage factors. If the general economic policy concerned itself with income distribution it would be interested in the value or cost of incentives designed to re-allocate labour, as such additional rewards would mean smaller increases for others, at least in the short run, although in the longer run the re-allocation could be expected to lead to a faster rate of growth which could provide the means for additional incentives to re-allocate or induce additional mobility if necessary. This could lead unions to take a greater interest in the whole question of mobility, including a discussion of future manpower needs, training requirements and so on. Steps to solve problems arising from these discussions would raise additional difficulties for some unions. Restrictions on entry to occupations can be significant aids to income bargaining; a fact appreciated by many professional groups, no less than trade unions. If unions are to discuss the relaxing of some of these restrictions, they will need reassurance that they are not being asked to make sacrifices just for the benefit of other groups, particularly employers.

If it is a condition of trade union co-operation that all forms of income should be brought within the policy, this means that trade union organisations must inevitably be brought into discussion of macro-economic issues. They must participate in broad general economic discussions ranging over such topics as investment levels, structural changes in industry and employment, regional development, source of investment funds, allocation of aggregate resources between various sectors etc. This will tend inevitably to widen the gulf between union leaders and the rank and file. Educational programmes will be necessary to bridge the gap and show why these subjects are of immediate concern and relevance to trade unions. Even if the incomes policy is a decentralised guideposts one, it will still be necessary for unions to participate in economic policy discussions. Failure to do so will mean that they will be unable to exert their influence on the basic policy conditions, e.g. should the rate of growth of all incomes be equal to the rate of increase of aggregate productivity, or should some forms of income receive preferentially high rates of increase? If there are to be exceptions to the guideposts, what are to be the criteria and how will it be decided when they should apply? Unions cannot leave these questions to others and they will not be able to discuss them satisfactorily without discussing other economic policy issues too.

Meaningful discussion of economic policy requires that the trade union representative can speak with some degree of

3*

authority on behalf of the trade union movement and their members. If they are constantly disclaiming such responsibility and stressing that they speak only in a personal capacity, their effectiveness will be considerably reduced. But, similarly, there will be strong pressures towards joint consideration of a wide range of economic and social policies, which currently might be regarded as the prerogative of government. If government is not prepared to discuss the broader economic policies, unions will not for long participate in an incomes policy. They will regard government's measures as undue discrimination against wages, for which no compensating changes are being offered.

Conclusions

The most important conclusion is that governments and employers must adopt a realistic attitude towards the contribution trade unions can make to an incomes policy. As voluntary democratic organisations, unions have to persuade their members to accept their policies. This places very real limits on the pace at which they can change and the direction in which they can move. Failure to appreciate this will merely lead to frustration.

The policy objectives must therefore be attainable. General economic policies must be co-ordinated. If economic pressures are too strong, unions and employers will be unable to induce the changes in behaviour that are required. Employers too have equal responsibility for ensuring that an incomes policy is implemented. Their actions can break a policy and demonstrate to workers that larger money increases are easily available. Employers' organisations no less than unions need to appreciate how far they can go and still carry their members with them. Unions will participate only if they receive offsetting advantages. It is doubtful whether promises to end or reduce inflation are sufficient. Other economic and social changes will be necessary and the policy must cover all incomes if it is to survive for long. Governments and employers have to decide how far they will participate in this.

The pressures towards centralisation, joint discussions and joint decision-taking will both provide the means for peaceful settlement of industrial and economic conflicts, while at the same time sharpening the areas of conflict by bringing them into the open. By providing the opportunity for discussion of differentials and income distribution, the policy will raise these issues publicly and there is a danger that the lack of fundamental agreement will be demonstrated. Industrial relations might then appear to worsen. However, the existence of a broad policy on these lines by necessitating a realistic appraisal of attitudes towards income distribution etc. is merely bringing to the surface issues which are latent and which have to be openly discussed if the economic problems of today are to be dealt with.

To change basic and deeply-rooted attitudes is a long process. Dramatic changes cannot be expected overnight. Temporary restraints may be accepted in emergency situations, but these cannot last. It is essential, therefore, that steps are taken to change attitudes on a long-term basis. This raises difficulties as there are sharp conflicts about what the "proper" attitudes should be. It must be recognised, however, that both parties will need to educate their members to the new situation. This must be based on some degree of common interest although, of course, differences can continue. The important point is that incomes policy is regarded as a long-term policy desirable in its own right. If it is not, then people will not make the required changes, and, when there are conflicts between the immediate demands of the policy and the preservation of some long-term interests, incomes policy will suffer. This may happen, for example, with the role of conciliation or arbitration. People must believe that incomes policy is both permanent and desirable before they will make the necessary adjustments to their behaviour. This means that governments must explain why it is in people's interests to have an incomes policy on a long-term basis.

CHAPTER 3

Trade Union Views on Workers' Negotiated Savings Plans for Capital Formation

I Introduction and Examples

The term "capital-sharing schemes" is a generic one covering a number of different types of proposals made in various Continental European countries. The schemes have certain features in common:

(i) they are intended to provide workers with the opportunity of accumulating wealth assets;

(ii) these assets are initially or primarily financed by the employer;

(iii) the amount of accumulation per worker is determined either by reference to the profits of the undertaking or in relation to the level of wages, or rate of change of wages, of the workers concerned. Essentially the schemes provide arrangements whereby workers receive some *future* benefits in the form of a monetary lump-sum payment or ownership of wealth assets from their employer. The capital contribution is also seen as a payment over and above the increase in *real* wages which would otherwise have been negotiated.

Arrangements which encourage workers voluntarily to increase their savings out of their own existing income, even though these schemes may include the payment of exceptionally large premia or preferentially high interest rates by the Government, or attract particularly high tax rebates or exemptions, are not generally regarded as capital-savings schemes. The distinction would become blurred were the employer to pay part of the premiums on workers' savings. For example, there has for many years been a law in the Netherlands providing premiums for savings financed by contribution from employers on behalf of their employees. These savings have to be frozen for a period of between four and ten years. The amount of premium varies with the length of the saving period but can be as high as 200 per cent. The contributions by employers are exempted from income tax and social security contributions.

Types of schemes

Capital growth sharing. A term used to cover arrangements whereby workers receive some share in the total "surplus" profits of the firm. "Surplus" means those profits remaining after deduction from gross profits of such items as taxes, depreciation, interest and a "reasonable" amount of dividends. The intention is that part of the ownership of all profits over and above a "reasonable" level shall pass to the employees of the company. The exact ratio in which the division between employees and shareholders takes place can be a matter of negotiation. As the intention is not to increase the disposable income of workers at the expense of retained profits it is the *ownership* of retained profits represented by share certificates which passes into the workers' hands and not the cash amount of their share in the retained profits. This means that the firm does not have to pay out any cash so its liquid resources are unaffected. It has to issue additional shares in itself which will have the effect of reducing the increase in market value of the existing shares which otherwise would have taken place as a result of the retained profits.

Additional Investment Wages

A concept developed, with some differences, in Germany, Italy and the Netherlands. It refers to arrangements whereby, after the normal direct spendable wage increase has been negotiated (as currently the case in ordinary collective bargaining), a second, additional increase is negotiated which cannot be currently received but is deposited by the employer on behalf of the workers in some form of approved savings. Although we have referred to two stages of negotiation the bargaining takes place simultaneously and the direct wage increase and the additional investment wage would normally be settled at the same time. In some proposals it is left to the free choice of the worker whether or not he takes all his wage increase in a direct form. That part going into savings as investment wages would receive specially high interest rates. In some schemes under the German DM. 312 Act,[1] the employer's contribution into savings deposits on behalf of the worker is conditional on the worker also voluntarily saving a smaller weekly amount. Failure to save voluntarily under these schemes means that the worker loses the employer's contributions; he has no choice of taking it as a direct wage increase.

With investment wages the employer has to pay out cash into the approved form of savings and therefore has to release some of his cash resources. The payments are "frozen" for some agreed period, e.g. five or seven years, to ensure that they do not lead to an immediate increase in consumer demand and a reduction in funds available for investment. The Italian proposals do not provide for a compulsory freezing period; it would be left to the voluntary choice of individual workers whether they saved or spent the investment wages.

Combined or Danish Scheme

The Danish LO has recently produced proposals for a scheme which combines features of both investment wages and capital-growth sharing. The amount of the employers' contributions is to be determined as a proportion of total wages, but payment in the case of limited liability companies and co-operatives is to be in the form of shares in the concern. Thus the *amount* to be received by workers is not dependent on the profitability of the undertaking but on the level of wages but, because payment is to be made in shares, there will be no pressure on the cash resources of the undertakings. Other parts of the economy, e.g. public sector and private companies, would pay their contributions in cash as in an ordinary investment wages scheme.

Examples

Capital-growth sharing. From the gross profits of a company certain "allowable" deductions would be made to cover such things as depreciation, interest and "reasonable" dividends. These could be decided by bargaining or laid down by govern-

---

[1] Now increased to DM.624.

ment. The remaining profits would be divided in some agreed ratio between employees and shareholders. If the actual dividends paid out exceed the "reasonable" figure, the excess would not be deductable when calculating the employees' entitlements. The division between employees and shareholders could be based, for example, on the proportion of wage costs to capital costs, and the division between employees according to their relative earnings. Other ratios could be determined. The company would hand over to a specially created Fund, cash or the equivalent in approved securities. The employees would then be credited with shares in the central Fund. There are a number of possible variations on this. The Fund could cover just one firm, or an industry or a region and so on. There are arguments for and against all the possible levels of organisation. If the company did not make any "excess" profits in a year there would be no capital-sharing payments. Workers would thus be taking a share in the risk of their company.

It might be assumed that any capital-sharing scheme would take the following broad form. From a figure of gross profits for a firm are deducted: depreciation, interest on loans and company taxation. From the resulting figure for net profits is deducted a minimum return on the capital employed. The remainder of the net profit is then divided between existing shareholders and employees. To determine the payment to the employees it is therefore necessary to determine the amount to be divided between employees and shareholders (which is referred to as Available Resources); and the proportion of this amount which is to be distributed to the employees (which is referred to as the Aggregate Workers' Share).

The formula used in the statutory French scheme is as follows:

$$\text{A.R.} = (Gp - t) \frac{5 \times k}{100}$$

$$\text{A.W.S.} = (\text{A.R.} \times \frac{W}{V.A.}) \times \tfrac{1}{2}$$

Where
A.R.   = available resources
A.W.S.   = aggregate workers' share

Gp   =taxable trading profits (trading profits subject to tax)

t   =company tax paid on trading profits

$\dfrac{5}{100}$ K   =shareholders' interest

K   =issued share capital, all reserves, and provisions which have been subject to tax

W   =total wage and salary costs

V.A.   =value added

It can be seen that in this particular proposal workers participate in only one half of the available resources after deduction of a 5 per cent dividend. There is no necessary reason why this should be so. They could participate in the full amount. Similarly the Distribution Ratio could be calculated in some other way. The French scheme is used above only as an illustration of one way of dealing with the various problems involved in a capital-growth sharing scheme.

There are obviously a number of "technical" questions to be answered with capital-growth sharing schemes which are based on the profitability of the company, which do not arise with investment wage schemes which take the amount of wage payment as the basis of calculation of workers' entitlements. These can be grouped under two main headings; firstly the calculation of the Available Resources, i.e. the amount in which the workers are to claim a share, and, secondly, the Distribution Ratio, i.e. the calculation of the amount to be received by workers both in aggregate and individually.

Available Resources. It is necessary to define profits and the first question might be to decide whether the basis should be the individual company, or, in the case of a multi-company group, the whole group. It has then to be decided whether all profits should be counted or whether profits from certain sources, e.g. activities outside the country concerned, should be excluded. Presumably some amount for depreciation would be deducted from gross profits, and interest payable on loan stock might also be deducted. It is possible to deduct interest on preference shares and then exclude the amount of preference shares from the capital base on which the "share-holders' entitlements" are calculated. It will then probably be necessary to deduct tax paid, and there might need to be adjustments made in respect of taxes paid on income received from overseas according to whether this was to be included in Available Resources or not. Finally it is necessary to deduct an allowance for shareholders' dividends and as this will most probably be calculated as a percentage return it is also necessary to decide how the capital base on which dividends are to be "allowed" should be assessed. For example, should the ordinary shares be valued according to their face value (assuming they have one), according to their average market value over some pre-determined time period, or according to some other formula? A Dutch report on the subject suggested that shares should be valued according to the intrinsic value as set out in the balance sheet. It is thought that if this were done there would be increased pressures to ensure that balance sheet values truly represented the value of the underlying assets. At the moment most assets tend to be undervalued in balance sheets. The choice between these possibilities could have a marked effect if market prices are generally higher than nominal values. It has then to be decided whether workers participate in all the remaining profits or in only a part of them.

The *Distribution Ratio* raises two main issues. Firstly, that of the aggregate workers' share, and secondly, that of the share of each individual. Proposals for the first often suggest a distribution based on the relationship of the total wage and salary bill to total value added. Alternative measures are of course possible. The second is often solved by distribution to each individual according to his particular wage or salary. Thus he would participate in the total aggregate workers' share according to the proportion of his wage or salary in the total wage and salary bill, possibly with some upper limit. The Danish proposals are for each individual to participate equally irrespective of the size of his salary.

Investment Wages

Trade unions would negotiate an ordinary direct spendable wage increase as they do now and in addition an investment wage. For example these might be a 4 per cent direct wage increase and a 3 per cent investment wage. The latter would be paid into a special Fund. Alternatively it might be left to the worker to decide whether to take the increase as wages or defer it for a stated length of time, say five or seven years (Italian proposals). To the extent that workers could, and did, take their investment wages in a spendable form it would not be possible to negotiate increases over and above the real direct wage increases normally negotiated. Otherwise there would be additional inflationary pressure. Preferential rates of interest and tax reliefs could be given to encourage investment wages. (There are a number of proposals along these lines on the Continent. In addition there are various schemes to encourage voluntary contractual savings in this way.)

Workers could be given the choice of having their savings deposited in various forms of approved savings, e.g. special investment trusts, Building Societies, and so on. With an incomes policy in operation one variation might be to say that wage negotiations were "free" but that increased over, say, 4 per cent, would be paid in investment wages which could not be cashed for a given number of years.

Who participates? It is thought that any worker in any type of employment can participate in an investment wages scheme but only those employed in profit-making concerns can join in capital-growth schemes. Thus, civil servants, for example, would be excluded from the latter. In fact it could be possible to devise a scheme which shared the "excess" profits of industry among all workers irrespective of their place of employment. This would considerably reduce any incentive effects the scheme might have. It would be possible to exclude certain groups. Those earning more than a given amount could be excluded completely, or permitted to participate only in a restricted way. In this way the inequality between lower-paid and very highly paid groups of employees could be narrowed.

Length of "freezing" period. All schemes must contain some provision for freezing the capital-sharing contribution for some time in order to avoid an increase in consumption and inflation. In some proposals the workers' shares are to be frozen until retirement, with exception clauses to cover such things as permanent disability. In other proposals the period may be five to seven years. There is a possibility that at the end of this period the unfrozen assets will be spent; on the other hand saving may become a habit and they may be left untouched. *Who controls the special Funds?* This depends on the scheme. In some proposals a joint employer/trade union committee would control them. In others the contributions have to be paid into certain forms of approved savings such as Building Societies, banks etc. and these organisations then control the funds deposited with them.

Compulsory participation? The Italian, Dutch and German proposals are for schemes which are voluntary in that it is left to unions and employers freely to decide to establish a scheme. It is not envisaged that the State should compel employers to participate. However the French scheme is a legislatively compulsory one.

Motives

(1) To redistribute wealth assets, and more particularly, future wealth assets.

(2) By creating a more equitable distribution of wealth to change future income distribution in a more equitable way.

(3) To find a way of accepting or even encouraging the need for industry to retain large amounts of profits for self-financed expansion, without also accepting that this should lead to increased wealth accumulation by existing share-holders, and without necessarily leading to more self-financed investments in the specific firms making high profits. This concept of "self-financing" regards industry as a whole and seeks to utilise retained profits to promote social and economic objectives irrespective of the particular place of their accrual.

(4) To reduce the inflationary pressure of wage claims which have as part of their object the redistribution of wealth or income in favour of wage and salary earners.

(5) To ease inflationary tendencies by encouraging increased savings.

(6) To increase the rate of future economic growth by encouraging investment.

(7) To provide an incentive to workers to improve efficiency in which they will now receive a share.

Actual Schemes

General characteristics	France	Netherlands	Germany
A. (a) Usual title	Participation of workers in benefits of expansion	Savings plans Investment wages	Capital formation
(b) Range	Enterprise	Industry	Industry
(c) Number of workers	2,392,205 in 5,4000 enterprises at 1.4.70 for 1968	25,000—printing industry 8,000—dredging	8,000,000
(d) Global amount p.a.	Varies 1–10% in practice.	1% yearly wages	624 DM per person.
B. Capital growth or investment?	Capital growth based on profits	Investment	Investment
C. Membership voluntary and compulsory	Compulsory	Compulsory	Varies
D. For I wage is employers' contribution to be matched by workers?	—	No	In some not in others
E. Freezing period	5–7 years	Until 65 years old	7 years
F. Type of securities	Shares and bonds	Any	Approved savings
G. T.U. control of securities	No, some funds placed in institution under T.U. control	Equal representation on Board	In some—T.U. bank
H. Worker choice of savings options	Collective agreement possible	N.A.	Yes
I. Government tax concessions	Yes	Not yet	Premiums instead— 30% p.a.
J. Comparable to concessions for voluntary savings	Yes	Voluntary schemes have concessions	Yes

Proposed Schemes

	Denmark	Italy	Switzerland
A. *General characteristics* (a) Usual title	Wage-earners' profits and investment fund		
(b) Range	All workers including public sector	Industry or firm	Industry (watch making and metal working)
(c) Number of workers	1·75 m	—	
(d) Global amount p.a.	½% rising to 5% but workers receive identical amounts from Fund	To be negotiated	Amounts available from participation funds
B. Capital growth or investment?	Investment wages	Investment	Investment
C. Membership voluntary and compulsory	Compulsory	Voluntary	Voluntary
D. For I wage is employers' contribution to be matched by workers?	No	No	No
E. Freezing period	5 years with exception—injury or retirement etc.	3–12 months	Retirement
F. Type of securities	Shares—limited companies and co-operatives. No limit for others	Shares and bonds	House construction
G. T.U. control of securities	Yes	Majority of Board	Joint
H. Worker choice of savings options	No	N.A.	No
I. Government tax concessions	No	Should be excluded from property tax and tax on dividends from fund	NK
J. Comparable to concessions for voluntary savings	—	Should be more favourable than general concessions	NK

(8) To change the balance of political as well as economic power in a more equitable manner, at the same time exerting social influences favouring the position of the individual in society. To democratise the power stemming from the ability to take large investment decisions.

Not all the objectives are advocated in every country. Some of them could, in fact, conflict.

The most important trade union objective is to secure a more equitable distribution of wealth and income. Unions are disillusioned with the results of orthodox collective bargaining over the past twenty years and so are searching for new ways of attempting to secure an effective redistribution. It is believed the proposals have one considerable advantage over the usual type of wage bargaining in that as they increase the workers' entitlements to income and wealth assets without also increasing their current disposable or spendable income they will not be inflationary as the additional "costs" to the employers (if this is how the employers' contributions are seen) cannot be passed on in the form of higher prices as aggregate demand has not increased. Against this it can be argued that if employers still regard their contributions as costs they will increase prices and the result will be higher unemployment. Alternatively governments' will have to expand demand in order to maintain the level of employment with inflationary consequences.

II Proposals and Experiences

The two tables show brief details of proposed and actual schemes in various countries. The answers have been summarised under the broad headings adopted as a guide for the discussion at the meeting. A short additional explanatory note is given for each country. A fuller account of the earlier proposals is given in the Report of the Florence seminar[2] and in the papers submitted to the seminar published in the Supplement to the Final Report.

------

[2] See "Workers' Negotiated Savings Plans for Capital Formation", OECD, 1970.

Netherlands

Proposals for both capital-growth sharing and investment wages have been made. Detailed studies of the possible economic effects and repercussions of various schemes have been made by the three trade union federations and also by the Social and Economic Council. The unions tend to favour capital-growth sharing as the preferable way of obtaining a share of future increments in wealth assets but have so far not been able to introduce any such schemes. The employers resist fiercely and some union members are not particularly interested in the schemes which contain this degree of uncertainty. In addition there are a large number of profit-sharing schemes already established in the country, which, while not providing the same element of participation as would the union proposals, nevertheless by providing some participation in profits probably reduce the pressure from rank and file members for more direct participation. Other profit-sharing schemes generally provide for the workers' entitlements to be paid in cash and therefore do not lead to the accumulation of wealth assets. Investment wages have therefore been negotiated in two industries and it is probable that this type of scheme will grow rather than capital-growth sharing.

An investment wage scheme was negotiated in the printing industry in July 1969. An additional 1 per cent of the annual wage income is to be put into a special fund on behalf of each worker. The contributions accrue to each worker individually and are frozen until the worker reaches the age of 65. Provisions exist for the payment of contributions before this date in the event of certain unforeseen events, e.g. disablement. The printing industry in the Netherlands has one of the best private pension schemes negotiated by the trade unions and therefore it would be wrong to regard the investment wage provisions as being no more than supplementary pension provisions. They are regarded by the trade unions as being a first step towards the accumulation of capital assets by the members.

The funds are managed by a Board consisting of an equal number of trade unionists and management which can invest the money in any securities it chooses. The investment wage scheme was introduced at the same time as a normal direct money wage increase was given so that the workers did not object on the grounds that this was a form of compulsory savings. However, some of the younger workers object to the freezing of funds until the age of 65 and would prefer to have access to them sooner than this.

It is thought that the union which represents workers in the paper industry other than printing will seek to obtain similar agreements. It may well be that other unions will then follow. There is an investment wage agreement covering a very small number of people in the canal dredging industry.

The Government is being urged to exclude contributions to investment wages from income tax and social security premiums. These are currently paid on investment wage contributions but are not paid on contributions made by workers to voluntary savings schemes. In these latter schemes, however, the worker pays a saving contribution from his after-tax income and it is the employer who is excused tax and social security premiums. There are certain additional tax-free premiums given by the Government, however.

Germany

There has been considerable discussion of wealth distribution in Germany since 1945. Voluntary savings are encouraged by special tax or premiums concessions and the unions have extended the provision of legislation to cover schemes established by collective bargaining. The first investment wage schemes in the construction industry required the individual worker to apply for participation through his employer and to make a small payment of two pfennigs an hour in order to receive the employers' contributions. Subsequent schemes in other industries do not require a contribution by workers. There has been a very considerable increase in the number of investment wage schemes and the number of workers covered by them in the past two or three years.

It is too soon to say whether the schemes have had any significant effect in redistributing capital assets either between employed persons and shareholders, or between different income groups among wage and salary earners and there has not yet been sufficient experience to determine whether workers withdraw all their savings at the earliest opportunity or whether they leave their past, but now unfrozen assets in savings deposits. Neither is it yet possible to say whether workers have reduced their other forms of savings to offset the amount of investment wages.

The DGB have rejected the proposals for statutory investment wages (Burgbacher Plan). They distinguish between two objectives:

(1) increased accumulation of workers' savings;
(2) providing workers with a share of the growth of the productive wealth of enterprises.

They believe that voluntary savings and investment wages will not play any significant part in redistributing wealth except perhaps in very special circumstances and to a very limited extent. While welcoming the extension of the provisions of the DM.312 Act and encouraging the voluntary negotiation of investment wages the DGB believe that the effective redistribution of future growth of wealth therefore requires some scheme of capital-growth sharing which allows workers to participate in the increases in profits. Thus voluntary savings and investment wages may further the first objective but are not considered as suitable for achieving the second.

Accordingly the DGB seeks legislation to establish capital-growth sharing schemes on a compulsory basis. Enterprises in the forefront of capital accumulation should be required to pay part of their profit to various funds which shall issue certificates in themselves to all workers. Limitations would be placed on the ability of workers to sell their certificates. This would provide workers with a share of future growth of productive assets as well as with increased savings.

Italy

CISL made their original proposals in the early 1960s for investment wages but although interest is still maintained in these proposals the scheme was not included as an item in the programme of action approved by the Congress of CISL in July 1969. This is taken to mean that while CISL is still interested in investment wages and will continue to seek to implement this at some stage in the future it is not one of their immediate proposals for action.

The CISL proposals were for investment wages on a voluntary basis so that individuals could choose to take all the increase in an immediately spendable form. The funds were to be controlled by trade unions and it was an important part of the proposals that this control would give unions economic powers not otherwise available to them. For example, they intended to use the investment resources to encourage regional development and thus use the investment funds to create an economic policy which they could not obtain by collective bargaining or by political pressures on Government.

The provisions of the Civil Code (Articles 2424 and 2429), dealing with the provisions to be made for the termination of employment, lay down that each employer has to set aside an amount proportional to the earnings of the worker to provide a termination of employment indemnity. During the period of employment the fund is, in fact, available to the employer for his own use. Thus some of the sources of funds for investment in Italy that are regarded as self-financed investment are, in fact, funds which are in a way the property of the workers. The use of these funds might be thought not to be different in principle from the use of funds accumulated under a contractual savings scheme. This would mean that the establishment of funds from contractual savings schemes, which could be used to finance investment, might not be regarded as such a dramatic departure from the traditional sources of supply of investment funds.

Denmark

The Danish proposals are recent in origin and were not therefore examined at the Florence seminar. They will be described in a little more detail.

The LO's committee on Economic Democracy at its meeting on 30th September, 1970, adopted "Principles for the Creation of a Wage Earners Profit and Investment Fund". These proposals were submitted to the Congress of the LO in 1971.

The intention is to establish a wage-earners' profit and investment fund by statute to which all wage-earners, irrespective of their place of employment, shall participate. All employers, private and public, shall contribute to the fund at the rate of 1 per cent of the total wages in respect of the first year of the scheme, increasing annually by ½ per cent until the contribution to the fund reaches a stable level of 5 per cent of total wages. The amounts paid into the fund and the interest and profits accruing to the fund from any investments it has shall belong to the wage earners in total but each wage earner shall share equally in the fund's assets. That is, although the contribution made by the employer on behalf of a wage earner is in direct proportion to the employee's wage or salary, the wage earner's share in the fund is not based upon his salary. The participation in the ownership of the assets of the fund is therefore absolutely equal for all wage earners, assuming that they have participated in employment equally. Unlike almost all other proposals, therefore, the wealth assets are to be divided equally and are *not* to reflect existing differentials in incomes between wage earners.

Individual workers are to be issued with certificates representing their assets in the fund. These certificates are not convertible but any individual can redeem his certificates from the fund after a freezing period of five years. Earlier encashment is possible in the event of death or disablement. The five-year period is a rolling period. Limited liability companies and co-operative societies will pay their contribution in the form of capital deposited in the enterprise as wage-earners' capital. That is, they must credit an appropriate amount of shares in the company to the wage earners, an amount determined by the proportion of wages due to be paid. In other enterprises part of the payments to the fund may, if the fund agrees, remain deposited in the enterprise as wage-earners' capital, or may be direct in a cash form. Wage-earners' capital in limited liability companies and co-operatives is to have a share in the total annual profits and dividends on an exactly equal footing with other forms of capital issued by the company. The proposals are seen as extending industrial democracy directly as well as extending economic democracy by the accumulation of wealth assets. Thus, in limited liability companies and co-operative societies it will be laid down that the wage-earners' capital shall be represented on the Board of the company by at least one member and by more than one member, if appropriate, according to the proportion of total capital of the company represented by wage earners' capital. At annual meetings of the company the wage earners' capital shall be represented by a number of representatives elected by all of the employees of the enterprise.

It is interesting that although the amount of contribution to wage-earners' capital is determined on the investment wage principle, i.e. according to the amount of wages paid and not according to the economic performance of the company, the provisions for limited liability companies and co-operative societies to pay their contribution in the form of shares in themselves incorporates a number of features of capital growth sharing. Firstly, it removes the pressures of shortage of liquidity which might otherwise be imposed on these companies. Secondly, and perhaps more importantly, it ensures that the wage earners will participate in the benefits of future economic growth and expansion.

Some estimates of the economic effects of the funds have been made on generally conservative assumptions, i.e. estimations that are relatively unfavourable to the development of the fund, e.g. that everyone will withdraw their capital immediately they are able to. Even so, it appears likely that after five years the fund will have assets of over 9 million krone, i.e. about 5 per cent of GNP and by the fourteenth year the fund's assets should stabilise out at about 12·5 per cent of GNP. As a proportion of their own company's capital, the wage-earners' capital will be about 5 per cent after five years, 14 per cent after ten years and 26 per cent after twenty years.

France

The French scheme was established by law under ordinances of 1967. As has been seen from the formula set out earlier, French workers are entitled to participate in one-half of the "excess" profits after meeting 5 per cent dividends, according to the ratio of wages to value added. (Note that 5 per cent for dividends after tax has been deducted is equivalent to a gross pre-tax dividend of 10 per cent.) Trade unions did not press for this scheme, which was introduced by Government and can be seen as an application of certain Gaullist views about participatory society which have a history of over twenty years. The unions vary somewhat in their reactions, some of them are reluctant participants in certain aspects of the scheme on the grounds that their members' interests will be better served if they take certain courses of action rather than if the unions abdicate all responsibility and refuse to participate.

The scheme applies to all enterprises employing more than 100 wage-earners. A little over 2 million workers are directly affected. The share of individual workers is proportional to their wage or salary in relation to the total wage bill, subject to a maximum of four times the ceiling used to determine the maximum amount of social security and family allowances. There are three forms of "reserves" or funds into which the workers' entitlements can be deposited:

(i) allocation of shares in the enterprise;
(ii) deposit in a fixed-interest form of blocked investment in the enterprise;
(iii) payment to a form of unit trust type organisation external to the enterprise, i.e. which covers more than one enterprise.

The method selected is determined by agreement between the employers and employees' representatives. To encourage voluntary agreement the freezing period of five years is extended to eight years in those cases where no agreement has been reached within twelve months of the end of the first financial year.

The GGT advised its members to select method (ii)—a blocked account with fixed interest in their own company on the grounds that this did as little harm as possible by guaranteeing the worker a fixed rate of return. The CFDT and FO on the other hand advised their members to select method (iii) and to this end have encouraged Inter-expansion, a unit-trust type organisation. They participate in the management of this body and are able to use the funds received to buy a variety of shares thus spreading the risk of capital gain or loss. Commentators appear to agree that method (iii) gives the workers greater benefits.

Enterprises receive tax concessions in respect of payments made under the law, or made voluntarily by companies employing less than 100 wage-earners. The amounts paid into the reserves are exempt from profits tax, which is currently charged at 50 per cent. Moreover companies are allowed to set aside for the acquisition of fixed assets an amount equal to the aggregate workers' share which is also exempt from tax. Thus by taking advantage of the investment concession companies can effectively obtain tax relief equal to the whole cost of the aggregate workers' shares, subject, of course, to the proviso that sufficient profits remain in the company after the deduction of the 5 per cent allowable dividends from net profits. If it has not proved possible to reach agreement with the employee representatives on the method of allocation of the workers' share the "penalty" on the enterprise is that only one half of the tax concessions in respect of investment provisions are allowed (the workers' "penalty" is the extension of the freezing period from five to eight years).

In effect the cost of the scheme is borne by the taxpayer (subject to the proviso above) and so there is no real burden on industry and thus there should be no inflationary pressure. Costs have not risen and there should not be any pressure to increase prices. The Government has stressed that the scheme is not intended to interfere directly with ordinary wage negotiation. Nor is it meant to give workers or trade unions any participatory rights in the decision-taking processes within enterprises. The scheme in no way affects the rights of the employer to take such decisions as he has previously taken. The provisions do alter the structure of trade union decision-taking in one way. The agreement between employees and employers on the method of allocation has been signed by shop-steward committees. The trade union representatives signing the agreement must be on the staff of the enterprise. In part the trade union federations were somewhat reluctant to participate in the processes, but employers seem also to have encouraged the making of agreements with shop stewards even perhaps to the point of encouraging their establishment where they did not previously exist (see *Le Monde*, 9th September, 1969).

It is difficult to assess the effects of the scheme so far. 1969 was the first full year of operation. A survey by the Ministry of Labour and Employment of fifty large firms showed that the average receipt was F317. The highest figures were F1,633 in the electrical machine industry, 1,388 in food and agriculture and 1,165 in chemicals (*Le Echos*, 15th December, 1970).

The results of a larger survey covering establishments of all sizes suggests that the figures are higher for larger firms. Of nearly half a million workers sampled who received more than 1 per cent, more than a half of them received less than 3 per cent of their direct wages, and only 11,000 workers in 15 enterprises received between 7·1 and 9·0 per cent. Other surveys suggest that probably a little over half the wage-earners concerned have their entitlements allocated to fixed interest accounts in their companies, generally receiving between 6 and 7 per cent interest. About 40 per cent have chosen method (iii).

The general impression is that the CFDT and FO are actively supporting Inter-expansion but many workers prefer the security, albeit perhaps lower rate of return, of a fixed interest blocked account in their own company. Perhaps this is not surprising. Workers have little knowledge and possibly considerable mistrust of financial institutions and the workings of the stock market, and even when the organisation is run by their trade union representatives suspicions will die hard. It will no doubt take some time in most countries before workers feel secure in this sort of activity (if it is desired that they should do so).

As we have seen, the cost is effectively borne by the taxpayer, yet both employers and trade unions give only grudging acceptance to the enforced introduction of the scheme. It is too early to say whether it will have any significant effect on wealth distribution, to some extent this will depend on the incidence of the taxes which might have to be raised to offset the tax exemptions granted.

III Trade Union Attitudes to Capital Sharing

Although trade unions are committed to a policy of redistribution of both income and wealth it does not follow that they support capital sharing as a desirable means of achieving these objectives. Some unions do not support a policy of redistribution of wealth by switching assets from existing shareholders to new individual shareholders, i.e. the workers. Instead they would prefer to see a system of state ownership of the redistributed wealth assets. There is a political or ideological distinction here between those trade unions that support state ownership or public ownership in its traditional forms, e.g. nationalised industries, and those trade unions which seek to redistribute wealth on an individual basis and would then have the individual workers, the new wealth-holders, group together in various forms of association, e.g. trade unions or a form of co-operative, in order to exercise collective power stemming from their individual small wealth holdings. This difference of opinion within the trade union movement as to the desirability of collective state ownership of wealth as the means of achieving a more equitable distribution of income and wealth reflects both a division of opinion as to the means by which trade union objectives can be achieved and in some ways a difference of opinion as to the ultimate types of society that trade unions are seeking to attain. A number of unions which are advocating capital sharing schemes would still regard themselves as working towards a socialist society but now see this being achieved through somewhat different forms of organisation than might have been the case in their programmes of say, twenty or thirty years ago.

Whether they support capital-sharing schemes or whether they advocate more traditional methods of redistributing wealth, trade unions appear to be agreed that existing methods of bargaining have been insufficient or ineffective in achieving their goals to any significant extent. In some cases the best that might be argued is that they have prevented any marked worsening of the situation. Some unions also believe that a wealth tax of an extent and severity that is tolerable, or that it is realistic to expect a government to introduce, will not, on the basis of past experience, make any significant change in the distribution of wealth. Other unions are more optimistic about the possible effects of a wealth tax.

In summary therefore trade unions take different positions regarding capital sharing because they have different views about the nature of society they are seeking to attain and different views about the most appropriate means of attaining it.

Type of Scheme

These trade unions that support some form of capital sharing generally believe that the most desirable scheme is a capital growth scheme. In practice, however, it has proved extremely difficult to establish this type of scheme by collective bargaining because of employer resistance, and therefore the schemes that have been negotiated have been of the investment wage variety. (The French scheme, which is a form of capital sharing, was of course imposed by statute.) Investment wages, therefore, tend to be seen as the first step in capital sharing because they are more easily implemented. However, these schemes are criticised by some trade unionists as being a form of forced savings. The fact that the investment wages are compulsorily frozen for some period of time is regarded as a form of forced savings that some trade unionists find objectionable. If there was no compulsory freezing period then, of course, the possibilities are that investment wages would not be additional to ordinary direct increases in spendable wages but would merely be a part of the ordinary wage increase. Supporters of investment wages reply to the accusation that they are fostering schemes of forced savings in two ways.

(1) The investment wage increases are, ideally, additional to the ordinary wage increases that would have been received anyway. Therefore they are not forced or compulsory savings out of what would otherwise have been consumable income but are additional gains which can, in economic terms, be received only if they are for some period at least frozen as savings and not translated into increased consumers demand.

(2) While the criticism of "forced or compulsory savings" might have some pejorative connotation, in fact there is nothing new or particularly intolerable about this. There are many forms of forced savings already, e.g. taxation and national insurance contributions. Thus it is misleading to criticise forced savings as such, rather one should look at the form the savings take, the object of them and who the ultimate beneficiaries will be.

It is, of course, extremely difficult, if not impossible, to determine whether investment wages really are additional to wage increases that would have been received in any event or

4

whether they are merely the ordinary wage increase received in a different form. It is probably the case that part at least of investment wages are wages increases that would otherwise have been received but also probably the case that part of them are additional to ordinary direct expendable wage increases.

Inflationary Effect

It is widely thought that investment wage schemes are more inflationary than capital growth schemes. This is because investment wages may be regarded as items of cost which require the payment of a cash sum which would otherwise reduce the company's liquidity and therefore requires the company to increase prices in order to replenish its liquidity. Capital growth sharing schemes could be inflationary if they were regarded as items of cost or that employers subsequently raised prices in order to make up for the value of shares they have transferred to workers' accounts. However, the Danish proposals appear to overcome the possible inflationary pressure of investment wages, at least so far as the limited liability companies and co-operatives are concerned by their requirement that the amount of contribution shall be paid in shares and not in cash.

From a union viewpoint the Danish scheme appears to combine the best features of both approaches. The amount of the workers' entitlement is determined by the wage bill and is not, therefore, subject to fluctuations according to the state of business and/or the trade cycle. However, because the amount to be paid by companies and co-operatives is not required in cash but in shares, in themselves these contributions ought not to be regarded as direct costs. There is no reason why the company has to raise prices to replenish liquidity as there has been no outflow of cash or liquidity. What has happened is that there has been an increase in the number of shares issued by the company but these do not in themselves add to these costs. The issue of shares, however, means that the workers will participate in the future capital growth of the company and in the future profits of the company.

In the other sectors it is still possible that investment wages will be regarded as increases in costs and lead to increased prices. It is, of course, obvious that if a prices and incomes policy is in operation there are more options open to contain the price increases.

On the crucial question of whether or not the schemes will be inflationary or whether they will actually redistribute income, trade unions in some countries believe that their proposals would not be inflationary. However this may be because they are as yet relatively small in coverage and amounts.

Basically a great deal depends on whether employers accept the redistributive objectives of workers' savings schemes. If they are prepared to see a redistribution of income and/or wealth then the schemes will be less inflationary than if employers are not prepared to see this redistribution. It is in order to prevent an effective redistribution that prices would be marked up. Or alternatively for some investment wage proposals that require payment of the workers' entitlements in cash form, it is in order to replenish liquid resources that prices would be increased.

Some unions which are at present uncommitted on the subject would support some form of proposals if they were satisfied that the scheme would achieve a greater degree of equity in the distribution of income and wealth without generating undue additional inflationary pressure. At this stage it is not possible to make any firm statements based on an analysis of evidence showing the working of various schemes and the practical effects as no scheme has yet been in operation for sufficient time. Even when schemes have operated for some time it will prove difficult to determine exactly what results came from the operation of the scheme and what economic results came from other parts of policy. Nevertheless there is a need, fully recognised by trade unions, for informed comment based on empirical surveys.

Power and industrial democracy

Some proposals are as much concerned with the effect the schemes will have on the distribution of power and decision-taking in industry as they are with the distribution of wealth in economic terms. For example the CISL proposals fully recognise that additional power affecting investment decisions would accrue to the trade unions as a result of their control over the savings funds. Indeed this is one of the major reasons their proposals have taken the form they have. The Danish proposals also see the scheme as extending a form of industrial democracy. Representatives of those employed in companies would, by statute, be offered seats on the Board of Directors to give expression to the views of the work force under entitlement resulting from the creation of shares in their name. This, it is suggested, would lead to increased participation by workers in the running of their company.

Some trade unions might reject this form of workers' involvement, while others would welcome it as preferable to a traditional form of public ownership. By encouraging worker participation at an enterprise level it may be possible to encourage a form of industrial democracy which would permit individuals to play some part in controlling their industrial environment. Other unions will prefer a more centralised system of state ownership and control.

A number of unions do not seek to exercise power directly through the control of investment funds which would accrue to the various organisations which would be set up with a capital sharing scheme. They would wish to be represented on the bodies but would not see that representation as providing additional power. Some unions are, of course, ideologically opposed to any direct involvement in share ownership as such, but often it has proved possible for unions to create special financial organisations to participate in this sort of activity if they so desire. For example the German trade union bank appears to provide services at least as good as those provided by other institutions and still reflect the particular value judgements of the trade union movement without becoming a direct subordinate institution of the DGB.

There are therefore two main threads running through the trade union discussion of power and democracy in this context. The first relates to power to influence investment or financial decisions as such, and this is, generally, advocated by trade unions which have not so far been able to obtain very much direct influence over economic decision-taking in their countries. The second relates to the participatory aspects of worker involvement in the running of their own enterprise which might result from the establishment of various institutions under capital sharing. These are seen as providing new or additional ways of achieving old objectives. They are opposed on the grounds that workers' control of industrial democracy should take other forms and that this particular form would, in fact, be harmful as it would divert workers from a more "full-blooded" type of socialism.

Summary

The differences of opinion in the trade union movement, which, on this particular subject, run deep, basically reflect two different approaches to the attainment of trade union objectives, as well as differences in the objectives themselves. Supporters of capital-sharing tend to be more willing to experiment with new techniques and methods, either because they recognise that they have not been particularly successful with older methods or because they have reinterpreted their basic philosophical positions, or their principles, to meet changed modern conditions. For example their view of industrial democracy and worker participation in a modern economy and their disillusion with state-run organisations may encourage them to press for workers' shareholdings and representative Directors. Critics, on the other hand, are suspicious of proposals which appear to be buttressing capitalism or the capitalist system. They believe that the creation of share-holdings for individuals will foster and sustain a "capitalist" mentality which will prevent the development of socialist philosophy and prevent the application of socialist policies based on state or communal ownership. Other critics, because they do not really believe that employers will agree to the handing over of real wealth assets, suspect that the end result will be additional inflationary pressures which will leave the workers as a whole no better off and may even worsen their conditions because of a reduction in the country's economic competitiveness. Criticism comes therefore from two beliefs; either the schemes will not work, or they will work "too well" and create many little capitalist-minded individual shareholders.

Perhaps somewhat surprisingly there is relatively little disagreement among those unions supporting the schemes that government intervention is needed to introduce proposals on a legislative basis or at least to provide conditions in which voluntary-negotiated schemes will be introduced. Even if it is desired to negotiate the schemes on a voluntary basis it is recognised that encouraging, albeit permissive legislation, would be of great advantage.

IV Conclusions

Clearly there are divergent views both within and between the various national trade union movements. Some will reject capital-sharing and investment wages on ideological and economic grounds. They seek to achieve their objectives in different ways, and more particularly through collective action, often State collective action. So far as these trade unions are concerned as long as they maintain their present policy position the various proposals referred to in this paper will have no attraction and, indeed, may be regarded as undesirable in that they could make it more difficult for collective action by creating small amounts of wealth assets to be held in the name of individuals. Thus these schemes will be seen, at best as irrelevant, and at worst as harmful.

Other trade unions will welcome these proposals or variations on them. They believe that new techniques are necessary to achieve certain basic underlying objectives of the trade union movements or that certain new methods of "individual owner-ship with collective exercise of power" arrangements are in themselves desirable forms of social and political organisations. Each national trade union movement may adapt the various underlying principles to suit its own conditions, priorities and objectives, and thus while it would be unrealistic to expect uniformity in the various proposals there will be common themes running through them. Generally they will tend to prefer capital-growth type schemes in that they are seeking to obtain control over the growth of profits and retained funds, but in practice they may find that employers are unwilling to negotiate anything other than investment wages.

It may be that the Danish proposals will, in time, come to be regarded as the most desirable way of dealing with this subject. They remove the major threat of inflationary pressure from the limited liability companies and co-operatives, although there is still the possibility of higher prices in other sectors. The amount of workers' entitlements is known in advance and not dependent on profit figures, although of course the future value of the shares in the Fund might well be influenced by the profitability of companies which becomes reflected in the market value of their shares in the Fund. By requiring payment in shares the scheme will ensure that workers collectively participate in the future growth of industry and do so in a way that is truly egalitarian. All workers will participate equally irrespective of their wage level, and the profitability of the enterprise in which a person works is not to be allowed to determine the amount of his capital entitlement. This prevents the inequalities in income resulting from differences in profitability of firms from being extended to differences in capital rights.

It is possibly the case that legal intervention will be needed to obtain effective capital-sharing schemes. Employers are unlikely to agree to them on a voluntary basis.

Given the growing interest in this type of proposal there seem to be very good reasons for keeping a continuing interest in developments in various countries. In a few years there should be evidence available to allow some assessment of the success of the various schemes, although this will be made easier if it is possible to persuade governments to produce better statistics on income and wealth distribution than is now generally the case.

The trade union representatives requested the OECD to keep this subject under review, and asked to be kept informed of developments. It is suggested that this can best be done through the auspices of the OECD.

In particular it was requested that the OECD should initiate studies of:

1. the implication of various capital-sharing and saving schemes for inflation and its control;
2. methods of ensuring a redistribution of income and wealth and the role these schemes might play;
3. review of statistics of income and wealth, including the intermediaries through which the statistics are collected and examined and proposals for their improvement.

It was also suggested that in future this subject be referred

to as Workers' Entitlement to Capital Growth Sharing, or
something similar, as the use of the term "Savings" might be
regarded as implying voluntary, or forced, savings from
existing income.

CHAPTER 4

Workers' Savings Plans for Capital Formation in Germany

Objectives of Workers' Capital Formation[1]

Discussions of capital formation for workers have taken place in Germany for more than fifteen years. Following the economic reconstruction, criticisms were made of the social results stemming from the economic measures. Opinion was expressed that while priority had rightly been given to economic redevelopment the social consequences were not entirely acceptable. The very success of the economic measures itself tended to foster this view, and the greatly improved economic conditions permitted, as well as caused, a shift in emphasis towards the social consequences of the economic success. In particular, it was felt that while measures initially taken to stimulate savings in order to finance investment were desirable, no matter that this led— or indeed inevitably did lead—to increased capital accumulation by the higher income groups, as these were the only parts of the private sectors effectively able to participate in savings to any considerable degree, as time went on the resulting uneven distribution of wealth assets became the target for criticism.

A more basic criticism was that the free market system did not appear capable, as currently operating, to effect a socially-acceptable wealth distribution. These views were expressed by trade unions, the Church, some politicians and academics. There was also a body of opinion that held that the existing methods of collective bargaining over money wages could not in themselves lead to a redistribution of wealth assets.

---

[1] The first section of this report which defined the various terms used in savings plans has been excluded. It appears in substantially the same form in the previous chapter.

Other views supported measures to encourage workers'
capital formation for social-political reasons, primarily in order
to defend a free market system. It was argued that structural
changes in the free market system, or changes in the results of
its working, were necessary in order to defend the system itself
and create conditions which would be favourable to the per-
petuation of social, political and economic democracy.

The objectives of the schemes and proposals for workers'
capital formation can be grouped under two main headings,
(a) economic and (b) social-political, although opinions held
by advocates do not necessarily fall into neat compartments or
classifications. Not all the objectives are advocated or even
necessarily accepted by each supporter.

(a) *Economic objectives*

(i) To redistribute wealth assets and particularly the future
growth of wealth, and to allow workers to participate in the
growth of productive capital, both to redistribute wealth and
in order to provide increased protection to workers' savings
during inflation.

(ii) By creating a more balanced wealth distribution, to
redistribute future income.

(iii) To increase total savings so that by freeing resources
from consumption there can be an increase in investment to
lead to faster and more sustained economic growth.

(iv) To reduce inflationary pressures by containing or
reducing the increase in consumption demand in money terms.
For example, if wages and consumption increase by 8 per cent
and productivity by 5 per cent there is likely to be a price rise
of 3 per cent. If money wages rise to 5 per cent, real consumption can still increase by 5 per cent with no price rise,
and if the 3 per cent "forgone inflationary" wage increase is
received as wealth assets workers have maintained the increase
in living standards and secured an additional wealth asset
formation with stable prices and inflation has been avoided.[2]

---

[2] It is accepted that this is an unduly simple and crude
model; for example, it ignores the impact of taxation on money
incomes affecting disposable income and assumes that the
marginal propensity to consume is constant. It ignores the

(v) To reconcile the reality of the importance of self-financing as a source of investment funds for many companies—indeed to allow this to continue although perhaps in a modified way—with the rejection of the view that self-financing should necessarily or automatically lead to an increase in the value of wealth assets owned by existing shareholders. This argument is an attempt to modify the working of a free market system to obtain certain social-economic ends without drastically altering the mechanisms of the system so that, for example, it is distinguished from proposals to prevent or reduce the incidence of self-financing. However, in some proposals the mechanisms of self-financing would probably be altered by the creation of funds initially channelled through credit institutions which could be returned to the enterprise. (This is discussed at greater length below.)

(vi) To provide workers with an incentive to improve efficiency in the fruits of which they will now share.

(vii) To facilitate the operation of an incomes policy.

(b) *Social-political objectives*

(i) To maintain the existing social order based on a free market system, by creating a society which exhibits the qualities of neither unbridled capitalism nor complete collective ownership.

(ii) To increase the freedom and power of the individual in a socio-political sense by providing him with increased economic security which provides a base from which he can exercise greater freedom of choice in such things as employment, housing, educational facilities for children and so on.

(iii) To effect a redistribution of decision-taking powers in industry as workers collectively exercise the rights accruing to

---

effects of market conditions and competition on price determination. It does not, however, imply any value judgements that prices *should* rise according to the rate of increase in money incomes or that the implied constancy of distribution between wages and profits is proper, fair or unfair. The model is presented only as a simple illustration of some of the reasoning behind some of the advocacy of workers' capital formation schemes.

them from their ownership of wealth assets and particularly their participation in ownership of productive capital through equities. They could also exert influence on investment decisions including the location of new investment through collective influence over the Funds, composed of the workers' capital entitlements. It is stressed, however, that this objective is not advocated by German supporters of capital formation. Workers' rights to participation are seen as guaranteed through co-determination, or its extension. Some advocates in other countries, however, particularly Denmark and France, may emphasise this objective very strongly.

Methods of encouraging savings and capital formation

Different methods of encouraging savings and, later, more particularly workers' capital formation, have been operative in the FRG. These can be grouped under three main headings:

(a) privileged treatment of expenditure for the purpose of savings under the Income Tax Law;

(b) encouragement of savings by the provision of premia;

(c) Acts to encourage the formation of capital by workers (Formation of Capital Acts).

Method (a) is an indirect encouragement in that it provides tax concessions and exemptions on savings while (b) and (c) provide direct encouragement through the payment of premia.

(a) Following the currency reforms of 1948 regular and lump sum payments to life assurance companies, payments to building societies and saving in respect of capital accumulation contracts received tax concessions. The contractual savings could take the form of a single lump sum payment frozen for a specified period or period payments on an instalment basis. Ceilings were imposed limiting the amount of savings that could qualify for tax concessions, originally on a fixed amount basis and subsequently as a proportion of income.

The tax privileges for instalment savings and general savings contracts were ended in December 1957 and 1958 respectively, and replaced by direct premium incentives. Construction savings continued to be eligible for either tax concessions or premia. In 1966 the changes were made so that there could no longer be simultaneous enjoyment of more than one type of incentive. Thus, individuals could no longer receive advantages under the House Savings Law and the Bonus Savings Law in addition to the special expenditure concessions for constructions savings. This step was taken towards harmonisation of the various schemes and also to reduce the budgetary burden of financing the various concessions and premia.

The higher income groups who fall into the higher tax ranges naturally benefit more from tax concessions than the lower income brackets. Thus not only do these groups have greater opportunity to participate in savings schemes but they receive larger effective returns from doing so. In the immediate post-currency reform period when the economic reconstruction received top priority this possible inequity was accepted as providing the most effective stimulus to total savings. It was only later as the pressures for urgent economic reconstruction reduced somewhat that other considerations could play more important roles.

(b) (i) *House Savings*

In 1952 the Law on the Granting of Premia for Construction Savings was introduced. This gave the saver the option of choosing the receipt of premia instead of the tax concessions in respect of certain forms of approved savings connected with house construction, the most important of which were deposits with building societies. There were various restrictions placed on the length of the savings period and on the use of the deposits as backing for credits or for assignment to a third party. Maximum amounts of savings which would qualify for premia were laid down and varied according to family circumstances. The rate of premium varies from 25 to 35 per cent according to family status, the maximum rate being DM.400. Moreover, savers with a taxable annual income of up to DM.6,000 (up to DM.12,000 for married persons) are entitled to a supplementary bonus of 30 per cent of the basic rate, so that the total of the basic bonus plus the supplementary bonus may amount to 45·5 per cent.

This Law was revised in 1969. The maximum eligible annual savings now ranges from DM.1,600 to DM.1,143 according to family status. The larger the family the smaller the annual savings needed to obtain the maximum bonus. In addition, since 1970 asset-generating benefits up to DM.624 a year under the Capital Formation Act, have ceased to count as part of the maximum assisted savings under this Act. The freezing period is seven years for building savings agreements and three years for house building capital accumulation agreements with housing undertakings or public authority housing authorities.

(b) (ii) *Bonus Savings Act*

A law on savings bonuses of 1959 replaced earlier special expenditure regulations. The primary intention was to avoid the undesirable consequences of encouragement of saving by tax exemptions (the higher the income the greater the advantage and persons not subject to taxation do not benefit from the concessions) and to introduce large groups of the population to the idea of saving and acquiring property. Under this law deposits may be lump sum or contractual instalments payments. The savings are frozen, although interest on them may be received and spent during the freezing period, while the saver usually has disposal of the bonuses only after expiration of such period. In 1963 the premia were graduated to be consistent with the Construction Savings provisions and the freezing period extended by one year, i.e. to six years for a general savings contract and to seven years for instalment contracts. The law was again modified in August 1970. The maximum permitted for savings to qualify for bonuses varies from DM.600 per year to DM.1,600 according to family status (benefits under the Capital Formation Acts excluded—see next section). Savings must not be directly or indirectly connected with any credit, in other words no bonus is paid if the savings were financed by means of a loan raised by the saver. There is, however, no penalty on premature repayment in the event of death or disability. From 1969 it has been possible, in certain circumstances, to transfer funds from a frozen savings account into securities, which are also frozen, without this being regarded as repayment.

Bonuses vary from 20 to 30 per cent. Further, a saver with an annual taxable income of up to DM.6,000 a year (up to DM.12,000 for married persons) is entitled to an additional bonus of 40 per cent of the basic bonus.

(c) *Workers Capital Formation Acts*

The first Act of 1961 was intended to provide additional incentives to the accumulation of wealth assets by workers by exempting workers and employers from social security contributions in respect of payments up to an annual maximum of DM.312 made by the employer to the worker for approved forms of savings to be frozen for a period of five years. The approved forms of savings were those qualifying under the Construction Savings Law or the Savings Bonuses Act for the construction or purchase of, or the repayment of a loan for, a publicly sponsored house, for the purchase of shares in the employers' firm at a preferential rate or as a fixed interest loan in the employee's name to the employer to be used in the employer's business and backed by a credit institution. The worker was also exempted from wage taxes on these payments if the employer had undertaken to pay such taxes in a flat rate of 8 per cent. The Act had little success. In 1964 only 380,000 workers with average savings of DM.263 benefited from this Act. The major weakness of the first Capital Formation Act was that it prevented an employer's contribution being negotiated as part of a wage agreement. Moreover a worker could participate only if his employer agreed to make a contribution on his behalf.

The second Act of 1965 remedied some of the weaknesses. The employer was freed from payment of the wage tax. More importantly, employers' contributions negotiated in collective bargaining agreements could now qualify under this scheme. The upper limit was increased to DM.468 for workers with three or more children.

Furthermore, it became compulsory for an employer, if the worker so requested, to invest part of his wages for him; moreover, the provisions were extended to cover public employees. Small firms with less than 50 employees were helped by a reduction of income or corporation tax equal to 30 per cent of the total of the employer's contribution on behalf of his workers or DM.800, whichever is the less.

The third Act, in June 1970, doubled the standard maximum ceiling to DM.624 without, however, raising the ceiling for families of three children or more. Instead the level of the

TABLE 1 *Maximum Possible Savings under Bonus Savings Act, House Savings Act and Capital Formation Act. Bonus shown per annum*

Family Status	Bonus Savings Act									
	Maximum in DM.			Percentage Bonus			Bonus in DM.			
	Basic (1)	Wkrs addi- tion (2)	Total (3)	Basic (4)	Extra bonus (5)	Supp. under CFA (6)	Basic (7)	Extra (8)	Wkr supp. (9)	Tot (1(
Single aged under 50	600	624	1224	20	8	30	244·8	98·0	187·2	530·
Married no children	1200	624	1824	20	8	30	364·8	146·0	187·2	698·
Married 1 or 2 children	1364	624	1988	22	8·8	30	437·4	175·0	187·2	799·
Married 3 children	1600	624	2224	25	10	40	556·0	222·4	249·6	1028·
Married over 5 children	1660	624	2224	30	12	40	667·2	266·9	249·6	1183·

NOTES

All examples assume that only one spouse is in dependent employment.

Columns 1 and 11 show the basic maximum savings which attract bonus.

Columns 2 and 12 show the additional ceiling of asset-generating benefits that can be held by workers under capital-formation investment wage type arrangements, i.e. these benefits do not count towards the permitted maximum savings under the two Acts.

Column 4 shows the percentage bonus under the Bonus Savings Act.

Column 5 shows the additional bonus given under the Bonus Savings Act to savers with low annual taxable income, e.g. for married persons or those living alone with one child the income limit is DM.12,000. Taxable income is calculated after deduction of various allowances, e.g. married worker with two children could earn up to DM.18,480 gross. Column 5 is in fact 40 per cent of column 4.

Columns 6 and 16 show the additional supplement obtainable by a worker from an arrangement under the Capital Formation Act.

workers' savings bonus was raised for these families. Until 1970 the workers were exempt from payment of wage and church taxes as well as of social insurance contributions on their investments. For workers saving the maximum amount the appropriate tax rate would have amounted in the majority of cases to approximately DM.130 a year (19·9 per cent wage and church taxes). Since January 1971, however, the tax and

| | | | | House Savings Act | | | | | |
| | Maximum in DM. | | | Percentage Bonus | | | Bonus in DM. | | |
sic 1)	Wkrs addi-tion (12)	Total (13)	Basic (14)	Extra (15)	Supp. under CFA (16)	Basic (17)	Extra (18)	Wkr supp. (19)	Total (20)
00	624	2224	25	7·5	30	556·0	166·8	187·2	910·0
00	624	2224	25	7·5	30	556·0	166·8	187·2	910·0
81	624	2105	27	8·1	30	568·7	170·6	187·2	926·5
34	624	1958	30	9·0	40	587·4	176·3	249·6	1013·3
43	624	1767	35	10·5	40	618·5	185·6	249·6	1053·7

Columns 7 and 8 are the appropriate amounts from columns 4 and 5 respectively applied to column 3.

Column 9 is column 6 applied to column 2.

Column 14 shows the basic bonus in percentage terms and column 17 in DM.

Column 15 shows the extra bonus for low income groups, but under this Act the maximum income ceiling of DM.12,000 applies only to married couples and not to single persons with one child as with the Bonus Savings Act. The extra bonus is 30 per cent of the basic bonus shown in column 14.

It can be seen that the two schemes work differently. In the Bonus Savings Scheme the amount of maximum permitted savings rises with family status while the House Savings Scheme decreases with permitted ceilings as the number of dependents rises but increases the rate of bonus so that large families need to save a lower amount in order to receive higher benefits.

social insurance contributions exemptions have been removed. Workers now receive a workers' savings supplement of 30 per cent of their asset-generating investments. This is raised to 40 per cent if the worker receives a tax allowance for three or more children. The maximum permitted is doubled if both spouses are in dependent employment. Workers with an annual income of DM.24,000 (DM.48,000 for married persons) do not receive the special workers savings supplement. Moreover, life insurance contracts are now admitted as an approved form of savings. Table 1 shows examples of the maximum permissible savings under the House Construction Bonus Act and the Bonus Savings Act with the workers' savings supplement under the Capital Formation Act. It can be seen that the maximum bonuses are considerable; always in excess of 50 per cent per annum in respect of savings under the Capital Formation Act when invested in one of the bonus-attracting forms.

This explains why the numbers of workers receiving asset-generating benefits on the basis of a collective agreement rose sharply with the coming into force of the third Capital Formation Act. In 1970 approximately 7·6 million workers received benefits under the third Capital Formation Act on the basis of a collective agreement, benefits that we regard as investment wages, and approximately 4·5 million benefited in another form from the provisions of this Act.

Other Measures

There are some other relatively minor provisions for workers' capital formation. They are minor in the sense that they have had little general effect and have not been widely implemented.

In 1967 an Act to provide incentives to joint stock companies, or limited partnerships with share capital, to issue shares to their employees was introduced. (The Act on Taxation in case of increased nominal capital out of company assets and on distributions of shares by companies to their own workers.) Companies can issue shares to employees below the market price, or generally accepted value, without the employee becoming liable for tax on the benefit accruing, provided that the difference does not exceed half the stock exchange price and that the gain from the market price difference does not exceed DM.500 per employee. The shares cannot be disposed of for five years.

The Federal Government has issued or sold shares in three important Federally owned enterprises to employees of the undertakings and generally to the public with limitations on the number of shares individuals could buy and as to the income of buyers.

The 1957 Investment Trust Act was regarded as providing

suitable investment opportunities for small savers, permitting them to spread their risk while receiving some advantages from investment in equities.

Proposals for Future Policy

The three main political parties in the FRG have all made proposals for introducing statutory provisions for workers capital formation. The Government (a coalition of the SPD and the FDP) has been working on a series of proposals prepared by four State Secretaries.

In outline the scheme provides for compulsory participation to run alongside the voluntary arrangements, including those collectively negotiated under the Capital Formation Act. The arrangement envisaged provides for a statutory levy on the profits of companies above a certain size or making more than a minimum profit. This levy would at first have to be transferred to a clearing house. The clearing house transfers the levy to investment funds which in turn issue investment certificates to the workers. The investment funds are decentralised and are integrated into the banking system. The worker receives the investment certificates from an investment fund of his choice. There would thus be workers' participation in the benefit of capital growth, as expressed through a formula for calculating profits.

Companies could pay their contribution in cash or in shares or other securities. The total contribution would depend upon the exemption limit on companies and the basis of the calculation of the levy, but might be in the region of DM.4,000,000,000 per annum, which, with say 20 million entitled workers, would produce an average amount of DM.200 a year. All entitled workers including those in the public sector would participate irrespective of the profitability of their own company.

The organisation of profit-sharing above plant-level would avoid the double risk of company-based profit sharing or capital formation schemes. The investment funds could sell on the open market debentures and shares issued by companies in payment of their contribution, if this is deemed necessary by the management of the investment fund.

In some ways the payment in shares rather than cash might be desirable, not in order to sell the shares but to increase the shareholdings of the investment funds. There is a general shortage of shares in Germany due to the relatively narrow base of the stock market, which would come under severe pressure if large amounts of cash funds in search of shares were suddenly to be released on the market. One reason for this narrow base is that in the entrepreneurial sector financing by ownership capital is relatively expensive and undertakings therefore prefer outside financing. It is envisaged because of existing tax regulations that tax reforms will change this position.

The opposition CDU-CSU favour a different, although still statutory compulsory approach. In the "Burgbacher Plan" they propose to introduce by law compulsory investment wages. This might be on a percentage basis (up to 1·5 per cent of wages according to this Plan) or on a flat rate basis as suggested later on. This would envisage investment wages of DM.20 a month (DM.240 a year) to permit the worker to participate in the growth of the productive capital of the economy. This would attract the 30 per cent government bonus under the Capital Formation Act. The worker would be free to choose how to invest his investment wages within the framework of an investment inventory limited to shares. It is recognised that the shortage of shares constitutes a problem so that measures must be taken to enlarge the supply of shares by changing legal provisions.

Investment wages are preferred by the CDU for two main reasons. Firstly, they believe that a worker's entitlement stems from his employment relationship and not from the fact that his company has made a profit of a certain amount. Secondly, they do not believe that only companies making profits should contribute as this would be regarded as a tax on success. Ordinary wages are paid irrespective of the state of profitability of the enterprise and so too should investment wages. The SPD/FDP Coalition rejects the payment of investment wages on a statutory basis for the following reasons:

(1) It compels the individual worker by law to make savings, while the project of the four State Secretaries does not involve any legal compulsion.

(2) It means fixation of wages by the State and thus encroach-

ment upon the collective bargaining autonomy of trade unions and employers' organisations who have already in many instances negotiated investment wages under the DM 624 Act.

(3) It creates a burden on public budgets, and thus on tax payers, amounting to more than DM.5,000 million annually.

(4) It favours capital-intensive large undertakings to the disadvantage of wage-intensive medium-size undertakings.

Attitudes towards these measures

In considering the attitudes of interested parties to the various measures and proposals for workers' capital formation it might be useful to refer to the measures under the three main headings.

(1) *Voluntary action by individuals.* This includes decisions by individuals, whether employed or not, to enter into a contractual savings relationship under the Bonus Savings scheme, the House Building scheme or for the workers individually under the Capital Formation Act. The tax concession for insurance, etc., can also be included. Essentially these decisions are taken by individuals who decide to benefit from the various government provisions.

(2) *Collective action.* This refers to investment wage schemes resulting from collective bargaining and attracting benefits under the Capital Formation Act and the other bonus or premia arrangements. The decision to introduce a scheme and the amount of the contribution are freely and voluntarily decided by the social partners in the course of their usual bargaining.

(3) *Compulsory measures.* The proposals of the SPD and the CDU involve compulsion as they would impose a statutory obligation on employers to contribute in one way or the other to workers' capital formation.

(a) *Government*

As we have seen, the attitude of government (as also the attitude of whichever party happens to be in opposition) has changed through time. The initial emphasis on voluntary measures and government inducements are now believed to be insufficient to effect the required degree of change in the distribution of wealth assets. Compulsory measures are proposed, not basically because they are believed to be desirable in their own right, but because it is not thought that even collective voluntary action will necessarily create more balanced distribution of assets. There is general recognition that a more balanced distribution is desirable to perpetuate the type of social order and free market system that is fundamentally accepted by both major political parties.

However, the government is aware of the budgetary burden of the payment of large sums as bonuses. This is one reason for some of the changes in the provisions governing the House Savings and Bonus Savings Acts.

(b) *Trade Unions*

The main German trade union centre, the DGB, has always accepted that an increase in workers' savings could provide an additional source of resources for investment, but has never accepted that the desired change in wealth distribution could be achieved by this means alone. At one stage the unions were of the opinion that collective bargaining might lead to sufficiently high wage increases to permit increased capital accumulation by workers but they now recognise that this is unlikely to occur. They now believe that institutional changes are necessary. Measures to increase voluntary savings are not opposed; indeed the DGB advocates greater bonuses for low income savers and always supported the payment of bonuses rather than tax concessions.

The majority of trade unions believe that investment wages do not solve the problem of concentration of wealth in the optimum or most preferred way. Some form of capital growth sharing based on profits is necessary to achieve this. Moreover, they believe that statutory investment wages conflict with the principle of autonomy in the economy in that it unduly restricts the freedom of the social partners to negotiate such settlements as they think fit. Further, they oppose investment wages where there is an element of forced savings so that the workers' living standards are lower in real terms than they would have been without investment wages.

Nevertheless, there has been a very rapid increase in voluntary collective agreements for investment wages. The first collectively agreed investment wages under the Capital

Formation Act were obtained by the Building Workers' Trade Union in 1965. George Leber, the President, had long advocated workers' participation in asset formation and indeed obtained his agreement with the employers somewhat in anticipation of the provisions of the second Act, which permitted collectively agreed contributions to qualify. A feature of the early schemes was that workers had to make a small contribution themselves in order to receive the employers' payment. Other unions and industries somewhat slowly followed suit but the major break-through occurred when the rank and file in the metal-working industry urged investment wages on a reluctant leadership.

However, the DGB does not oppose inter-firm profit-sharing on a compulsory basis, and have advocated this for some time. As do most trade unions, they emphasise that the scheme should be on an inter-firm basis; schemes confined to individual companies are seldom welcomed by trade unions. Also they do not believe that statutory profit-sharing interferes with the autonomy of the social partners, in the same way, as it does not prescribe that certain features should be part of their wage settlement.

They are strongly opposed to any suggestion that any form of capital-sharing should be part of any form of incomes policy which would result in lower real wage increases. Neither do they favour any incomes policy on the United States or the United Kingdom guidelines approach. Similarly it is not the intention of the DGB to use any of the power that might accrue from capital formation schemes to exert any additional pressure during wage negotiation; for example, they reject the possibility of denying credits from the Funds to firms which pursued wage policies considered undesirable by the unions.

The unions are quite firm that they do not wish to use workers' capital formation in order to obtain greater economic or political power for themselves through the control of the funds. They draw a sharp line between asset formation and co-determination. This is one of the reasons that the DGB advocate a decentralised system of Funds rather than the creation of a single Central Fund which would control all the resources accruing from employers' contribution. They also accept the use of the existing credit institutions, although additional ones might be created as well. But they effectively own one of the large banks and credit institutions and so are well able to compete for workers' funds in a free choice situation.

They do not favour any proposals that investment wages or other forms of wealth accumulation should be used as economic regulators. Thus they do not approve of reducing the freezing period during a downturn of the economy in order to stimulate consumption. If such action was successfully implemented it would necessarily prevent the accumulation of wealth assets by workers and this is repeatedly emphasised as the major purpose of such proposals.

(c) *Employers*

The employers have been concerned with capital formation for two main reasons; economic conditions are such that the increasing investment requirements should be met by the freeing of resources from consumption, and, on social and political grounds, it is believed that the free market order can continue only if many people are able to participate and accumulate capital. The problem is seen as essentially that of encouraging more savings by all sectors of society, but particularly the lower income groups, and of redistributing future capital growth in a more balanced way.

Three principles underly the employers' approach.

(1) There should be an individual decision by the person concerned to want to form capital assets by refraining from consumption.

(2) There should be willingness on the part of those providing the means and on the part of those investing them.

(3) Measures for capital formation should not impair or threaten monetary stability, economic growth or full employment. The various goals of economic and social policy should be co-ordinated.

Within the framework of these principles they believe that the existing savings schemes need additional encouragements to induce more voluntary saving, and to give more positive incentives to lower income groups. Although initially they opposed the inclusion of benefits under the Capital Formation Acts in collective agreements, in October 1968 they changed their policy and joined the unions in supporting this type of agreement. Two of the reasons why their attitude changed were that they initially thought that collectively-agreed capital formation schemes might be unconstitutional (the Court ruled that they were not) and they were concerned that investment wages would be additional to ordinary direct wage increases and impose an intolerable burden on industry. They do not hold this view to the same extent, certainly in relation to voluntary collective schemes. However, they do believe that German industry could not bear the burden of compulsory profit-sharing and voluntary collectively-agreed investment wages. They observe that there is still scope under present legislation to extend the coverage of the schemes. They also believe that existing collective schemes could be improved without embarking on a completely new approach.

Profit-sharing schemes on a voluntary basis are not opposed. The dangers of "double risk" are recognised and ideas are being considered whereby it might be possible to create investment trusts for funds from single-firm profit-sharing schemes, so that the risks would be spread. Also it is recognised that the declared aim of creating conditions in which workers can participate through voluntary action, on either an individual or collective basis, in productive capital, requires additional supplies of equities. The shortage of equities is seen as a danger in both the SPD and CDU proposals.

In short, the employers support measures to encourage voluntary capital formation—individually or collectively—and would strengthen some of the inducements. However, they strongly emphasise the importance of schemes being voluntary. Within a voluntary system they prefer investment wages to profit-sharing. The social partners are used to negotiating about wages and should continue to operate in a field in which they have demonstrated their capabilities. The employers' acceptance of capital formation measures is based on hard realism rather than altruism. They appreciate that industry needs large investment funds and recognise that if these were obtained through prices and profits there would be social unrest and a threat to the system. A social order based on consensus requires a broadly based ownership. They oppose statutory provisions because this would result in undue interference in the freedom and autonomy of the social partners and because they fear that levels of participation might be set which would exceed those regarded as tolerable by the people actively concerned in taking decisions in industry, with possible dangerous consequences for capital growth, full employment and price stability. They emphasise that if these goals are to be safe-guarded it must be recognised that capital accumulation by workers is a long-term process which cannot be satisfactorily dealt with by essentially short-term measures.

(d) *Credit institutions*

Banks and credit institutions have an important role in the German economy, in part resulting from the general reluctance of companies to raise finance by the relatively expensive method of issuing new shares. Moreover, they have established strong positions in workers' savings schemes through the operation of the various laws to encourage savings. Naturally enough they are extremely strong advocates of the continuation of the freedom of choice by individuals to decide how they wish their capital contributions to be invested, within the framework of choice laid down by government.

Both commercial banks and savings banks therefore support all measures to encourage savings and the accumulation of wealth assets by all sections of the community. If there is to be a statutory scheme the banks would prefer that the existing structure and methods of competition should be preserved as much as possible. They would propose a clearing agency to collect and distribute funds to workers. Companies could pay in cash, shares or IOU's. These could be converted into money and the agency would give cheques or credit notes which would be deposited in the institution selected. They believe that the various encouragements have some effect in changing the propensity to save, although it is appreciated that reliable evidence is not fully available.

Discussion of objectives

It was not possible to produce collective conclusions about the effectiveness of the German schemes and proposals or about schemes generally. In this section therefore we shall raise some of the issues which we believe to be important to a study of workers' capital formation. We shall try to provide different arguments reflecting different points of view, without coming down on one side or the other.

(a) *Redistribution of wealth*

The main question is whether schemes for workers' capital formation do lead to an effective redistribution of wealth or income. The experience of the schemes so far does not provide any satisfactory evidence in this respect. Until 1969 the schemes were on the whole on an individual voluntary basis and were predominantly used by the higher-income groups. It is not possible, therefore, to extrapolate the net economic effects of the results of individual saving in the early 1960s to the widespread application of schemes or the extension of the collectively bargained schemes. However, it does appear to be the case that the provision of government-financed inducements to encourage individual voluntary savings does not have any significant effect in increasing the savings of the lower-income groups. It is predominantly the medium and high wage and salary-earners who take advantage of these voluntary schemes. Moreover it is possible that the net effect of the schemes could be contrary to the declared objectives. If the benefits of the schemes, and in particular the receipts from bonuses and/or tax incentives are received mainly by the higher-income groups and the tax system is not sufficiently progressive, then it may be that the lower-income groups are in effect financing the savings efforts of the medium- and higher-income groups. The degree of progressiveness of the tax system and the actual incidence of utilisation of the voluntary savings inducements will determine whether there is any effective net redistribution of wealth or income and if so, in which direction this is. It would appear that in the past the effective net redistribution has not been as significant as might be desired and we understand that this question is currently being considered by the German government. It is a problem that is also under consideration in other countries.

The question of whether there is any effective redistribution can be looked at from three aspects:

(1) Is there a redistribution in real terms or are employers' contributions matched with price increase? Are the schemes inflationary?

(2) Will workers continue to maintain their holding of wealth assets once the freezing period is over?

(3) Is the total net result of the schemes that workers generally finance their receipts of bonuses from the state by additional tax payments or by foregoing other state provisions, i.e. is there a high opportunity cost to workers?

Inflation

The question of whether schemes are inflationary can be considered at two levels. The first is the analysis of the immediate consequences of the schemes in terms of employers' pricing policies. The second is any subsequent policy decisions taken by government in the pursuance of other economic goals in response to any immediate reactions of employers. It is the second approach which gets behind the immediate surface of the schemes to try and assess the effects of the full collection of attendant government policies and the reaction of groups and individuals, that is the more important, but it is the first type of assessment that creates the possible conditions in which the second might occur.

Firstly, it was generally agreed by the German representatives that employers would try to pass on any additional cost, as they perceived them, into higher prices. Thus investment wages would be regarded as additional costs, as ordinary wage increases are. Whether these could in fact be passed on would depend on conditions in the product market. The greater the incidence of uniform investment wages in a single industry the greater the possibility that firms in that industry would feel able to increase prices, subject to the strength of foreign competition, and this will vary from industry to industry. Supporters of voluntary schemes who are concerned over the inflationary aspect of investment wages stress that the employers would not willingly agree to excessive amounts as they would be aware of the threat to the product market. This is the normal position in collective bargaining. However, it has to be recognised that the mere fact that employers do agree to investment wages voluntarily in collective bargaining does not necessarily mean that these will not lead to higher prices any more than the fact that they agree to higher direct money wage increases does not necessarily mean that these too will not be passed on in higher prices. Bargaining conditions may result in settlements that add to inflationary pressures. It cannot be assumed therefore that acceptance of a scheme denotes acceptance of transfer of real resources or real assets.

Some supporters of investment wages reply that macro-economic analysis can show that inflationary pressures will not result, as investment wages are different from ordinary wage increases in that they do not lead automatically to an increase in total disposable income on the part of workers and that therefore total demand in money terms cannot rise sufficiently to maintain real demand with higher prices. Thus investment wages are seen, in aggregate terms, as a way of increasing labour costs without increasing money demand, thereby avoiding additional inflationary pressures.

Two counter-arguments can be made. Firstly, it is possible that workers will reduce voluntary savings elsewhere once they have investment wage assets, thereby permitting an increase in total money demand for consumption goods which would allow prices to rise. Secondly, firms might still increase prices, with a fall in total real consumption demand and consequent un-employment. Or some firms in some sectors—perhaps those more protected from foreign competition—might increase prices with the same result, depending on the various elasticities of demand. If employment is reduced the government might be obliged to intervene to maintain full employment and stimulate real growth. According to the measures adopted to stimulate the economy it might be that prices would be per-mitted to rise thus effectively allowing the investment wages to be passed on in higher prices. In this case either there could be no effective redistribution, or there would be greater monetary instability, or both.

It may be that schemes based on profit-sharing or some other form of capital growth are more difficult to pass on as there are no predetermined fixed amount of "costs" to cover. On the other hand it could still be possible for firms to increase prices to raise additional profits to cover their contribution. However if they succeeded they would automatically increase the amount of the workers' entitlements. This could mean that if firms sought to maintain the absolute level of profits available for shareholders' ownership, total profits and hence prices would have to rise by more than the amount necessary to cover the immediate workers' entitlements. The additional increase necessary would be determined by the reciprocal of the employers' share in profits.

For schemes to be non-inflationary, therefore, it is necessary that they do not lead to an increase in consumption through a reduction in the savings ratio of disposable income and that the "costs" are not passed on in higher prices. It is possible that the second condition has a better chance of being met if the employers' contribution is levied not in cash but by the issue of additional equity shares. There is thus no need for the company to obtain additional liquid resources, and their ability to finance investment would be unimpaired. This would also provide workers with a share in the productive capital and avoid the difficulties involved when the normal stock market base of equities is narrow. Even here, however, there could be some price effect if companies seek to maintain the same *level* of dividend payments to private shareholders, as the total equity base on which dividends have to be paid would be increased.

In the absence of general price controls, there does not appear to be any guarantee that workers' capital formation through investment wages or capital growth sharing will not lead to additional inflationary pressures, either directly, or as a result of subsequent government action to restore the level of employment. The crucial features could well be the specific policies adopted by governments if there is a threat to the level of employment. In so far as discriminatory active manpower policies can make a contribution to stimulating the economy in a less inflationary way they would appear to be preferable to general measures to increase the level of demand. However it has been argued that the dangers of inflation are such as to reduce the desirability of these schemes, particularly on a compulsory basis.

There may also be some inflationary pressures at the end of the freezing period if workers then spent their unfrozen assets. Thus it might be that there would be a significant increase in demand for durable consumption goods. There is some evidence about the behaviour of those who saved under the Savings Acts which suggests that the great majority continued to save their unfrozen assets. However this is not particularly good evidence about the way in which workers might behave when their assets under Capital Formation Act agreements are unfrozen, as the early savers were in the middle and higher income groups and had chosen voluntarily to save and could therefore be assumed to have relatively strong propensities to accumulate wealth assets. It is too early to say whether workers will change their propensity to save as a result of these schemes but clearly the ultimate success of the measures hinges on this.

However some advocates of the schemes believe that there is no particular danger from the spending of unfrozen assets if the schemes continue on a roll-on basis, one year's contributions being paid as one year's savings are unfrozen. Thus it is not the case that in year 8, assuming a seven year freezing period, all the accumulated assets can be disposed of, only those from year 1 which have been frozen for the full seven years, and these would be offset by the savings in year 8. Even though the actual savings in year 8 might be less than the amount of savings in year 1 plus generous bonuses, the net effect could be the same if the government levied taxes in year 8 to finance the payment of the bonuses on year 1 assets. From a macro-economic view this will depend on whether the contributions in year 8 are additional in real terms to the wage increase that is then received in relation to the increases that would otherwise have been received, and of course on the path of the economy and the government measures taken to offset any inflationary tendencies or pressures on employment levels in the preceding years. There is insufficient reliable evidence to form a firm view on this aspect and the probable consequences are un-certain. Trade union opinion believes that there will probably be changes in workers' propensity to save by retaining their assets in wealth form.

There is also some disagreement on the basic concept of wealth distribution. Some believe that the normal measures of wealth assets are misleading in that they tend to exclude workers' ownership of accumulated pension rights and con-sumer durable goods. They believe that if these were included workers would be seen to have greater holdings of assets than a study of savings, house ownership and the possession of shares, etc., suggests. While inclusion of such items would also increase the total wealth holdings of the higher income groups, possibly by a larger flat amount, it is probable that the relative proportional differences in wealth ownership would be reduced were the other items to be included. In particular, employers point out that the self-employed tend to have smaller, or no, rights to benefit under state pension schemes so that some of their apparent private ownership of wealth is really in lieu of equivalent "hidden state-provided" assets possessed by workers.

Even without an appropriate definition of wealth it is clear that this is a relevant issue to all discussions of workers' capital formation. There is a general view that it would be desirable to have improved statistics on wealth ownership, saving ratios of different groups and the effects of state schemes, although there is less agreement about the specific priorities.

The tax effect

To the extent that schemes are regarded as a tax they may have inflationary repercussions in the same way that other apparently anti-inflationary measures prove to have inflationary effects. The repercussions on wage bargaining from the price effects can perpetuate any initial inflationary shock. Some of the Group take the view that this is no different from, say, an indirect tax on commodities as part of an anti-inflationary policy, while others believe that it is more inflationary because of its effects on the capital market and the implied reduction in dividends or rates of return.

Some believe that from one point of view these schemes have the same economic effects as a tax on company profits, or a tax on companies based on their wage bill, with the benefits of the tax returned to workers. In this case it might be argued that a general tax could be levied and the returns to workers could be made on a more discriminatory basis with increased benefits going to the lower income groups. The distribution of the tax proceeds could be carried out in association with existing social security provisions, increasing their progressiveness and deepenging their redistributive effect. Alternatively government might announce that the proceeds of the taxes will be subsequently returned to individuals in lump sums in order to provide them with the greater economic security and freedom advocated by supporters of capital formation schemes.

Supporters of capital formation tend to reply that this misses the social and political parts of their proposals. While it may be that there would be similar economic results in terms of redistribution there would not be the immediate transfer to workers of the ownership of assets and they would not have the same freedom of choice to decide how they wished to invest their entitlement. The social aspects of the schemes have been strongly emphasised by some members and they would clearly not regard a tax and social security alternative as satisfying their demands for workers to be able to participate more effectively in decision-taking. The creation of private ownership of assets is considered important in its own right.

German opinion is particularly insistent that workers' savings schemes should be in addition to the present broad and far-reaching social security provisions. They argue that workers' capital formation would only be meaningful if seen as a second step towards greater equity, the first step being a considerable income redistribution through social security schemes. They would not regard it as an alternative.

Thus the example of the Italian termination funds, whereby employers must make contributions to a fund from which workers receive payment when they leave that place of employment was not regarded by some advocates in the Group as a satisfactory variant of capital formation schemes. The worker has no control or influence over the use of the funds during his employment, indeed they are in the control of the employer. They are not regarded therefore as providing satisfactory elements for the satisfaction of the social aspirations of advocates of workers' capital formation.

There is no consensus as to whether schemes will lead to a more balanced distribution of wealth. It is agreed that the secondary repercussions and resultant policies of government must be taken into account when considering this question. The issue might be simplified into the question of whether it is possible to give workers additional wealth assets without there being an increase in the workers' savings ratio and the ways in which this can be achieved. Some believe that there has to be a deliberate decision by workers to save more and refrain from consumption. Others believe that it is possible to transfer assets to workers out of the savings, or the forced increased savings, of others. Thus schemes for workers' capital formation are seen as essentially a transfer of the ownership of assets. Supporters of schemes believe that this is the only really effective way of creating ownership for workers, as their incomes are generally too low to permit the necessary amount of savings on a voluntary basis that would be needed to make any significant impact on the total wealth distribution. Thus voluntary savings are not condemned but regarded as insufficient to solve the problem. Against this it has to be decided whether the existing owners of wealth will agree, even perhaps reluctantly, to transfer the ownership of part of their assets, current or future, to workers. Schemes are therefore being devised which make the process as painless as possible to companies, or which make evasion as difficult as possible, while at the same time the external economic effects on inflation and growth are minimised.

(b) *Investment*

In a market economy, or a mixed economy, full employment requires that there be sufficient profit opportunities to induce employers to take decisions which create employment, although public investment too will play its part. This implies that there are large profit opportunities, or at least that the rates of return are such that employers or those responsible for providing investment finance choose to invest in employment-generating activities in the country concerned rather than in other forms of investment or investment in other countries. This may create a situation whereby the amount or the share of profits in national income that would stem from the rate of profitability on investment necessary to induce the appropriate level of investment to maintain high employment would be regarded as socially undesirable. Capital sharing may be one solution to this problem in that it would allow the ownership of part of the profits in national income to be more widely spread. This will depend upon whether those responsible for taking investment decisions and for supplying investment funds, and these can be either or both professional managers of companies or individual shareholders, differentiate in practice between the desirable rate of return on investment and upon the return to individual providers of investment finance.

To the extent that part of the expected return to shareholders includes capital gains or appreciation of the value of their shareholdings in addition to dividends, and this may be due to differential tax rates on dividends and capital gains, then even measures to transfer some of the ownership of wealth assets to workers while maintaining the rate of dividends to ordinary shareholders may create problems. The more that we assume that existing stock exchanges and money markets reflect a general state of equilibrium of risks and returns, current and discounted, the greater disturbance or distortion we should expect from the introduction of capital-sharing schemes. This might affect either the money market and the associated credit institutions, or might also affect real investment in productive capital.

The latter will be affected for example if the resulting rates of return (including capital appreciation on equities) between equities and other forms of assets, changes, so that new finance for investment is not forthcoming. Even though an economy may rely relatively little on new issues as a form of investment resources for productive capital there could still be adverse effects if shareholders insisted that they receive the total available profits as dividends as they no longer chose to reinvest back in the company through self-financing. Under some schemes this would of course automatically also increase the receipts of the workers funds as they too would receive interest on equities held by them. But the overall effect could be to reduce the supply of resources available for productive investment. It may be that if there was a marked switch towards non-equity paper the resulting changes in relative rates of returns might induce some investors back to productive capital assets.

There would most probably be disturbances in money markets and relative rates of return in any case. The increased supply of funds, or paper, or both, can be expected to change existing relationships. Whether this is considered a serious or a relatively minor matter will depend in part on the view one takes regarding the present functioning of these markets and their allocative mechanisms and in part on the priorities one accepts in social and economic policies. But as we have stated previously there is recognition in Germany that the existing base of equities is too small to provide adequate supply of participation in productive capital for the large amounts of workers' funds becoming available. This has to be dealt with if the aim of increasing ownership of productive capital, as opposed to other forms of capital and wealth, is to be achieved.

Some fear that the dilution of the rights of existing equity owners and the reduction of the total effective returns on investment in productive capital implied in schemes might have the effect of driving capital abroad. This will depend on the degree of balance of total return and risks in investment projects in different countries and the sensitivity of investment proposals to location. Some believe that the effects of some schemes could be particularly marked within the EEC while others pay more attention to the total labour unit costs, or anticipate greater harmonisation of schemes in the Community.

Although there have been differences of opinion on the direction and strength of the possible effects on investment, there was no disagreement that this is an important issue. There were different views as to the possibilities open to government to implement corrective action should adverse tendencies in investment develop.

There is wide agreement that the best way of extending additional protection to small savers against inflation is by creating conditions in which they can participate in the growth of productive capital assets. In this sense there is a desire to change the qualitative nature of workers' savings assets. Even though it might be possible to provide additional protection by the payment of large bonuses this is not considered as satisfactory as actual participation in inflation-protected assets. Nevertheless it is appreciated that if schemes are introduced, the economic consequences of a downturn in the economy could be even more widely felt than is currently the case, as the nominal market value of workers' savings assets could well fall. There is no way open to government—and it is debatable whether if there is it should be adopted—whereby workers can both participate in the growth of productive capital assets and not bear the usual attendant risks of such investments. This raises the question of whether workers are psychologically prepared to accept these risks. Some hold the view that workers prefer certainty, and indeed that small savers ought to do so.

The fear might also be expressed that by building-in protection against inflation to workers' savings, governments might be less resolute in their anti-inflationary policies. While some people might hold this as a general proposition there was nothing in our experience in the Federal Republic to raise concern that this might occur there. The general disapproval of inflation was such as to minimise this danger.

(c) *Effects on Institutions*

The widespread adoption of either of the proposals for statutory schemes, and indeed as the remarkable growth in collective investment wage agreements has had, will inevitably cause some changes in the working of the credit institutions. There will be significant increase in the amount of extra funds coming on to the market. The sheer bulk of these funds cannot but increase the collective power of the credit institutions even though as a result of the operation of competitive forces in the credit market there may not be the emergence of any excessive monopoly power by a single institution. If there are tax reforms which make external financing more attractive to companies the role of the credit institutions might be expected to become more important as providers of equity capital. This too will increase their power.

The credit market might also be affected if government issues additional paper to cover the costs of paying the bonuses. It may be that some of the current contributions might be loaned to government for this purpose but we would expect there to be some change in government credit both in amount and quality as a result of the schemes.

The collective bargaining institutions will also undergo some change. We believe that a statutory scheme will inevitably influence bargaining as the statutory obligations will be raised in negotiations as a relevant factor governing the ability of companies to grant current improvements in terms and conditions of employment.

The trade unions will, with either scheme or merely with the continuation of the present large-scale voluntary agreements, need to continue their considerable educational work so that their members are able to exercise the freedom of choice given them. Their success in this task will, in our opinion, ultimately have consequences on attitudes to the economy generally which might be expected to reflect themselves in wage bargaining.

(d) *Power*

The advocates of capital-sharing schemes in the Group, particularly the trade unionists in relation to their own countries, emphasise the role of these schemes in transferring to workers and their organisations powers of decision-taking and of influencing the development of the economy. This may be expressed by stressing the social purpose of schemes, which implies that workers should be given a greater degree of participation in the management of their enterprises. To some people this is more important than any effects there may be on the total savings ratio and the provision of additional resources for investment. There are differences of view as to whether there should be a single Central Fund or whether there should be a number of decentralised funds operating as far as possible within the framework of the stock exchange and current credit institutions and practices. But the attachment to the participatory element must be stressed if we are to present a fair picture of these attitudes.

As we have pointed out earlier this does not play a major role in consideration and advocacy of schemes in the Federal Republic. The German view emphasises that the legislative provisions for co-determination were the appropriate vehicle for furthering workers' participation, if further extension be considered desirable. They are quite clear in their approach that capital formation schemes are not intended to provide additional participation in management decision-taking. There has been considerable disagreement with the German view on this question. This no doubt arises from the different legislative frameworks within which capital formation schemes are advocated and introduced. There is already legislation in the FRG which deals with participation and there appears no need therefore to use the economic measures to obtain additional decision-taking powers. This issue has been approached directly. It may be that in some other countries the participatory aspects of capital formation is emphasised because there are no alternative provisions available. Thus the differences arise, in part at least, from the different environments.

But there may also be differences of opinion regarding the desirability of creating large powerful organisations which could exert considerable influence and seriously change the existing structure and balance of power and influence. In this respect it may be that opinion in the FRG is more cautious about creating very strong organisations than are similar interests in some other countries. The DGB and the white-collar federation, the DAG, both emphasised their mistrust of very powerful organisations in this sense, even when these are controlled by trade unions. Thus although the DGB have a trade union bank in which they hope workers will invest their capital entitlements they accept the "rules of the game" that if workers freely choose not to do so there is nothing they can or should do about it except increase their competitive attractiveness within the credit institutions.

Having expressed these differences in approach, and recognising that the specific policies adopted in each country will reflect both the realistic aspirations of groups in each country and the particular environment existing there, we should not seek to express preferences outside our own individual countries. But we should emphasise that the degree of preference given to the social rather than the mainly economic elements and objectives will obviously play a major part in determining the type of scheme that is introduced and the institutional arrangements and provisions will express these aspirations and priorities as well as dealing with the realities of the situations in each country. Thus, for example, if there is a long tradition of self-financing and tax provision discouraging the raising of external finance it is unlikely that a scheme will successfully be implemented which seeks to switch to external financing overnight. There must be a whole series of changes introduced contemporaneously in order to change attitudes and practices and induce action along the new desired lines. It is to be expected therefore that the kind of schemes that might be introduced will vary from country to country.

Final Note

The problem of the distribution of wealth is a crucial one for the continuation of our type of societies. Increased voluntary savings by workers are recognised as providing one approach, but there are disagreements on whether this can ever effectively solve the basic problem. There are differences of opinion on the desirability of compulsory schemes. There are differences on the complete economic repercussions of schemes but agreement that these should be considered in terms of the ultimate realities rather than the immediate superficial effects.

There is agreement that further studies and discussions of various schemes and their results would be beneficial to all and that improved statistical information about savings, the trend in savings ratios and the distribution of wealth (although there are problems of reaching agreement on the definition of this) should be sought. Schemes for workers' capital formation will no doubt increase in number, coverage, and intensity, and more countries will consider measures.

CHAPTER 5

Capital-Sharing Schemes

These notes are intended to provide a brief statement of some of the arguments pro and con capital-sharing schemes. They are neither exhaustive nor conclusive.

Redistribution of wealth

Orthodox collective bargaining can do little, if anything, to redistribute wealth in a more equitable way. It could only hope to do so if it were possible to obtain wage increases at the expense of profits and the additional wage increases were saved. If they were not saved there would be no wealth redistribution although the rate of wealth accumulation might be reduced, as would the rate of investment. Essentially the object is to transfer the ownership of increments in wealth from existing wealth-owners to the employed population. The stronger the desire to redistribute wealth the weaker the objections to "freezing" workers' entitlements; this stops the "savings" being spent.

Against

In the case of investment wages the major criticism is that there will be no redistribution of wealth. Nor will income be redistributed. The scheme will also be inflationary. If it is believed that employers (this term will be used to cover those responsible for making wage and price decisions in companies) will be unwilling to see part of "their" wealth assets and capital-growth pass to workers they will regard investment wages as they do ordinary wage costs and seek to pass them on in the form of higher prices. If it is not possible to pass them on because of a highly competitive market which includes foreign firms not subject to capital-sharing they will refuse to concede these additional increases. It may not be accidental

5*

that the first industry to negotiate some sort of first approximation to a capital-sharing investment wage in Germany was the Construction industry which is relatively immune from foreign competition in a protected home market. What will happen therefore is that workers will be forced, by higher prices, to reduce their level of real consumption, and in return receive some wealth assets in the future. It will be a type of forced savings.

It might be replied that the fear of inflation is excessive. There is a great difference between an increase in labour costs resulting from investment wages and one resulting from an ordinary wage increase. The former does not automatically result in an increase in workers' purchasing power. It is not therefore possible for companies to pass on the higher costs without suffering some loss of sales. If this is so then employment will fall. Thus it might be that investment wages will lead either to faster inflation or more unemployment. However, as no Government can for long tolerate very large increases in unemployment, measures will have to be taken to stimulate the economy which will automatically create conditions in which the higher costs can be passed on. The inflation will therefore appear; it might be delayed a little on the way. The argument that capital sharing cannot lead to inflation is based on assumptions from aggregate analysis which might not hold in practice.

While it is more difficult to pass on the cost of capital-growth sharing it is still possible that companies will seek to minimise the impact by increasing prices. Although this will lead to a corresponding increase in profits, in which the workers will share, it will depend on the ratio of distribution of profits whether it is possible to reduce the effective capital transfer to workers in this way. If it does there will be danger of inflation or unemployment.

The basic criticism is this; if companies do not wish to see part of their profits pass to workers they will seek to pass on the costs in higher prices. This will lead to inflation. If it does not it will lead to unemployment either as some firms can no longer afford to stay in business or as some firms see a reduction in demand for their products as a result of other firms increasing their prices. The choice is therefore between inflation or unemployment. If unemployment increases significantly the government can be relied on to increase demand. This then creates conditions in which costs can be passed on and so inflation continues.

In defence of capital sharing two points can be made. Firstly, if firms are not prepared to see a transfer of profits in the form of wealth assets to workers why do they agree to capital sharing? However the same question could be posed in relation to orthodox wage bargaining. If firms do not intend to increase wages at the expense of profits but merely to increase prices why do they agree to an ordinary wage increase? Secondly, if wealth cannot be redistributed, as opposed to confiscated, by capital sharing, what other way is there? There may be weaknesses in these proposals but are there any better ones which also offer the advantages claimed for capital sharing?

The existence of a prices and incomes policy can limit the opportunity of companies to pass on the costs of capital sharing in higher prices. To the extent that this is done there can be a redistribution of wealth.

Redistribution of income

As wealth ownership provides income, a redistribution of wealth will lead to a redistribution of future income. Assuming that the total rate of wealth accumulation does not alter, this redistribution will result in a net transfer of income from the shareholders to the employed, unless the wage increases negotiated are less than they would otherwise have been in real terms. Trade unions generally are committed to a redistribution of income between wages and profits. It is very unclear whether they are able to achieve any substantial redistribution through the mechanisms of orthodox collective bargaining over wages. By and large, wage increases are passed on in higher prices maintaining the wage/profit ratio, are covered by higher productivity, or, ultimately, lead to the firm going out of business with a subsequent loss of employment. So long as trade unions try to redistribute income through collective bargaining—and we are uncertain as to the quantifiable effect of this motive—there is obviously a danger of additional inflationary pressure.

It does not follow that it would necessarily be a desirable objective for trade unions to succeed in redistributing income away from profits. To the extent that a large amount of investments is financed out of retained profits any increase in wages at the expense of profits will lead to a reduction in the amount of resources available for investment, unless dividends are reduced. The increase in consumption could also generate inflationary pressures. Thus there may be considerable conflict between the aims of the redistribution of income and the maintenance of the rate of investment, if done through higher direct, spendable wages, but not if done through capital-sharing schemes which preserve the investment ratio.

Against

There will be only little redistribution of income as the amount of wealth redistributed each year will always be less than the total increase in wealth that year. Existing methods of taxation and social security measures are a better way of achieving a more equal income distribution. Further, as the marginal propensity to consume of the employed population is greater than that of shareholders, it will be necessary to ensure that they do not consume all of the future income accruing from their wealth if inflationary pressures and an undesired switch of resources from investment to consumption is to be avoided. This switch will probably take place in any event as shareholders seek to maintain their previous standard of living by eating into wealth.

Retained profits and investment

The need for self-financed investment has been referred to. It does not however follow that because industry currently retains large amounts of profits to finance expansion that this is either a desirable or efficient way of obtaining economic growth. There is one difference with capital-sharing schemes; under some arrangements it may be possible to reduce the *incidence* of "self-financing". Although the same amount of investment could be "financed" from undistributed profits it does not necessarily follow that this need be self-financed by the company itself. It may be possible to transfer the retained profits to other firms which are in greater need, or to firms whose expansion is more in keeping with some other aspects of economic and social policy. Thus if companies had to pay over part of their retained profits into a central Fund, those responsible for running the Fund could decide whether to lend back the contribution to the company concerned. Through their powers to make loans or provide investment funds they would be able to change the allocation of resources. This would, of course, depend upon the contributions being in cash. If companies were given the option of paying in shares the only degree of influence would be in respect of the future income earned by the Fund on shares already in its possession.

Against

Companies would not willingly agree to a scheme which made them pay their contributions in cash. Even if they were willing to see part of the ownership of retained profits and future capital growth pass to workers they would not be prepared to see the control over the company's own profits do so. Professional managers might be less concerned with giving up ownership of part of retained profits but much more concerned to maintain their own control over their use. In any event there is no evidence to suggest that some other group of people would take better investment decisions. In particular, if trade unionists were on the committee concerned it is likely that the decisions would be much more conservative and cautious. Also they might be tempted to take decisions on social grounds. While this might be praiseworthy from some viewpoints it might be undesirable from an economic growth aspect.

Inflationary wage claims

To the extent that wage claims are attempting to redistribute income or wealth towards wages, capital-sharing schemes could lead to a lessening of the inflationary pressure as this objective is met outside the negotiation of ordinary wage increases.

Against

It has already been pointed out that the inability of companies to pass on the cost of capital sharing depends upon an aggregate analysis and an acceptance of unemployment and, for some firms, loss of business, or even their collapse. In practice these restraints will not operate. It is not known to what extent wage claims are based on a desire to redistribute wealth. If this is not a major motive there will be little easing of inflationary pressure.

Encouragement of savings

It has been argued that schemes will lead to more savings on a number of grounds. As workers become used to saving, albeit in a compulsory way, they will decide to save more out of their current income. If the schemes are successful and lead to less inflationary pressure it is possible that the real wages can rise at the same speed, and savings increase as future growth of real incomes is greater. The reduction of inflation could encourage people to save; the present situation discourages saving as price increases destroy the future value of savings.

Against

If workers are forced to save they will reduce their voluntary savings. The ultimate effect therefore could be to reduce the aggregate level of savings with a corresponding undesirable increase in consumption. If on the other hand companies try to pass on the costs, and inflation is increased, there will be an even greater disincentive to voluntary savings.

Economic growth and investment

Economic growth could be speeded up in two ways. There could be more investment as people reduce current consumption. Secondly, the investment resources could be allocated in a more efficient way as the reduction of self-financed investment and the pooling of retained profits over wider areas could lead to better investment decisions.

Against

The possible effects on faster growth through a better allocation of investment resources has been discussed above. There is no evidence that trade unions, or any other body which might control the Funds of a capital-sharing scheme either wishes to, or is competent to, control the investment resources in a way more suited to faster growth.

Incentives to efficiency

Under a capital-growth scheme workers would share collectively in all the profits over the "reasonable" amount for their company. They would thus have a strong and direct interest in increasing the efficiency of their undertaking.

Against

Experience with existing incentive schemes suggests that the greater the coverage of the scheme the less the incentive effect. These schemes would be company-wide in coverage and therefore have little if any incentive.

Power

The existence of large cumulations of wealth undoubtedly give political as well as economic power to those controlling them. This point is particularly stressed in Germany. It may be that the countervailing power resulting from a capital-sharing scheme will be exercised by representative organisations on behalf of workers, e.g. trade unions and could be the basis for a form of participatory industrial democracy which gave to workers and their representatives power over investment and resource allocation decisions.

Against

Economic power can be better tackled by other means, e.g. wealth tax. Capital-sharing schemes are unlikely to make much impact on accumulations of power for some time as they are concerned only with additions to wealth assets and not with existing wealth. Moreover, it is preferable, if one wishes to tackle the question of power, to transfer it to the State which can deal comprehensively with all proper interests, not just the sectional interests of trade unions.

Economic arguments against

Reduction in investment

If it is thought that the present combination of dividends plus capital appreciation is a fair, or even an economically justifiable return to investment, then it may well be that capital sharing would lead to a reduction in new investment. As part of the total return would be taken from investors they might decide it was no longer worth while undertaking investment, particularly investment in new projects which contain some risk element. This could be the very sort of investment that ought, from a growth viewpoint, to be encouraged.

This may be true. If it is, it also means that it is not possible to redistribute income in any way that affects the total return to shareholders. Thus the limits of taxation on dividends must have been reached, so also must the limit on company tax and on capital gains tax.

It might be necessary to draw a distinction between those shareholders who purchase existing shares—which has no direct effect at all on the level of real investment in plant and equipment—and those who subscribe to new issues, i.e. those who release some resources for real investment. The former group can take action which might affect the relative yields on different types of securities leading, if the scheme is successful, to a general reduction in interest rates. The latter group are in a better position to affect the rate of new investment. This can also be influenced if the former group of shareholders insist that the company pays out a larger proportion of retained profits.

Balance of payments

This could be adversely affected in two ways. There could be a deterioration on current account if prices rose following the scheme. On capital account, domestic investors might seek to invest abroad where no capital-savings scheme was in existence. If one assumes that the international capital market is in some sort of equilibrium at the moment a reduction in the total return on domestic investment would have this effect.

Other arguments against

No real change

One of the most serious criticisms of these schemes is that they do not lead to any real change in the distribution of meaningful economic assets. The redistribution of wealth is merely a change in the nominal ownership of share certificates. Workers are not allowed to convert their "wealth assets" into current consumption as this would be inflationary. What they are able to do therefore is frame their share certificates, hang them on the wall and admire them.

The validity of this point applies equally to all proposals to redistribute wealth. The distinction between wealth and income must be clearly drawn. Ownership of assets can change hands with no economic effects resulting from the change of ownership. (Qualifications to this are considered below.) If the wealth is converted into consumption at a different rate from what would otherwise have occurred there will be economic effects. This is just as true for a proposal for a wealth tax as it is for capital sharing.

Psychological

Far from the scheme improving attitudes and leading to an easing of inflationary wage pressure the proposals would actually worsen workers' attitudes as the element of compulsory savings would be so strong as to swamp any beneficial reactions.

In reply it can be argued that it is not possible to know what the reactions would be to such a scheme as it is so different from anything currently in force.

Concentration of risk

It is sometimes argued that it is wrong for a worker to invest his savings in the company which employs him as he becomes too dependent on the success of one firm. A scheme whereby his wealth assets were tied to the firm which also paid his wages would therefore be undesirable.

This comment is in part misplaced. If it is assumed that the scheme covered more than one firm so that a unit-trust type arrangement exists, then although the worker's *entitlement* to wealth assets might be determined by the same firm paying his wages the security of his accumulated assets are not.

Capital-Sharing Schemes and Incomes Policies

Collective bargaining about wages (including fringe benefits, etc.) is concerned with the distribution of income either between wages and profits or between different groups of wage-earners. This is equally the case whether the wage claim is "defensive", i.e. seeking to obtain an increase to compensate for price increases which have taken place since the last settlement, or to restore a relativity altered by some other group, or "offensive", i.e. seeking to increase real wages either by relation to some change in productivity or on other grounds or to deliberately change relativities. Similarly, price increases can be seen as concerned with income distribution, e.g. if wages increase and prices are not increased there is a redistributive effect towards wages. If the wage increase is equal to the productivity increase a zero price change maintains income distribution and is one reason why firms may be willing to match productivity increases by wage increases but grant higher increases only if price increases seem feasible. It may be that action taken to redistribute income towards wages in one sector in fact leads to a redistribution between sectors if profits through price increases and product demand elasticities are such as to cause some other industry to decline as demand is maintained in real terms in the initial industry.

There *may* be differences between the attitudes of trade unions (considered as identical with workers at this stage) and price-makers who need not be considered identical with shareholders. This identification and differentiation of interests between the two groups may not in fact be so clear-cut or valid but it can provide a working hypothesis. Wage-earners want to change income distribution so that they can either increase current consumption or increase their wealth assets. Price-makers want to increase or maintain their share of income so that they can satisfy shareholders' demands for current consumption and wealth accumulation through dividend payments but also because they wish to have retained profits for self-financed investment. One approach to capital-sharing rests on the belief that it is possible to differentiate the two aims of price-makers and take action which will satisfy the objectives of wage-earners. If it is possible to transfer the ownership of some of the retained profits from shareholders to wage-earners then it may be that some of the inflationary effects of the interaction of wage claims followed by price adjustments may be avoided or reduced.

Capital-growth sharing is seen as the purest way of doing this. The workers' entitlements depend on the residual after meeting the "proper or allowable" first charges on gross profits. It is argued that the scheme cannot therefore be inflationary as attempts to increase profits in order to maintain the same amount of retained profits to be owned by the shareholders as they would previously have owned must inevitably lead to a larger amount of wealth assets passing to the workers, and would therefore be self-defeating. However, this may be true in terms of proportionate shares in retained profits, shareholders' claims can rise only if workers' shares rise, but if shareholders exercise pressure on price-makers to maintain the same amount of retained profit per private shareholder's share there could be an upward inflationary push, the magnitude of which would depend on the ratio of gross profits to turnover (the measure of profits to price per cent sold) tax rates and the relative shares of retained profits going to shareholders and workers.

With investment wages the position is less clear in principle. The employers' contributions might be seen as a charge on the "excess" retained profits and thus represent a genuine transfer of the ownership of wealth assets from shareholders to workers. On the other hand, there may be a greater possibility that they would be regarded as additional labour costs in exactly the same way as direct wage increases and passed on in price increases. This danger might be emphasised by the fact that investment wages are fixed irrespective of the profitability of the enterprise or industry in any particular year. a feature which is one of the attractions to trade unions as it reduces the risk element.

If it is accepted that it may be possible to differentiate the interests of the price-makers or managers from those of the shareholders, then there may be grounds for believing that capital-sharing might create opportunities to redistribute income and wealth in ways other than by normal wage bargaining. The income redistribution would occur in two ways. Firstly, future interest or dividend receipts from accumulated workers' wealth assets, and secondly, by changing the normal definition of income so that investment wages or capital-growth contributions are included. This change in the definition is important. Critics of capital sharing might argue that income distribution appears to be log-normal over very long periods of time in many countries, so that attempts to change the distribution are doomed to failure. Even if this is so, on the accepted definition of income it does not follow that the distribution of income plus wealth asset accumulation is either log-normal or constant through time. Indeed, it is known that the distribution of wealth is neither log-normal nor constant.

From the viewpoint of an incomes policy, the key question might therefore be "Will workers accept this new definition of income and be prepared to see their wealth assets accrue from capital sharing rather than by attempting to redistribute through orthodox collective bargaining methods?"

Much depends on the underlying objectives of workers. It is possible that the equating of workers with trade unions might be wrong. Trade unions certainly express concern over wealth distribution and seek in their policies to redistribute in favour of their members. However, it is possible that the members themselves are far more interested in the redistribution of income in that their basic objective is to increase their current level of consumption. If this is so, then capital-sharing schemes will be less likely to lead to an easing of money wage demands. Even so, it is possible that although in the early stages trade unions favour capital sharing more than do their members, experience of schemes will lead to a demand for them by workers. There appears to be some evidence that this has happened in West Germany where the number of workers covered by some form of investment wages is now in the region of seven million and trade unions which previously were lukewarm to these schemes have negotiated them as a result of pressure from their members.

One of the areas where there may well be greater initial agreement between trade unions and their members is that of the treatment of profits in an incomes policy. It is widely believed that incomes policies are tougher on wage incomes than profits and the distinction between profits and dividends is appreciated by trade unions much more clearly during an incomes policy. Current dividends may be frozen but retained profits can always be paid out in the future. Moreover, as many incomes policies are initiated during difficult economic circumstances when the general level of profits may be somewhat low, the growth in profits following the recovery of the economy appears to be particularly unfair. This is exaggerated if part of the general economic programme associated with the incomes policy is a stimulation of investment to obtain faster growth, and the investment is primarily financed from retained profits. There can often be a built-in conflict in the total economic policies. In order to obtain the agreement of trade unions to some degree of restraint in money wages it is necessary to ensure that other income groups do not gain by this restraint and yet the other aspects of policy may require or involve an increase in other incomes. This may be for investment or it may result from an increase in exports where prices may be rising in order to match world price levels.

The Scandinavian models of income distribution and inflation rest on the assumption that if prices in the competitive or world trade sectors rise faster than domestic prices would, given the internal wage settlements and productivity growth, the increase in profits from exporting would lead to an unacceptable redistribution of income. Internal wages therefore rise in order to maintain factor shares in the higher profits from exporting. Other wages in the economy then rise accordingly. It may be that in situations where domestic prices are rising less quickly than international prices there may be less demand for an incomes policy. If, however, an incomes policy is still sought, it clearly becomes necessary to tackle the question of income distribution, and particularly the growth in profits in the exporting sector. Export levies might be one way, but capital sharing might be an alternative. The general conclusion, however, is that trade unions are increasingly reluctant to see what they regard as adverse developments elsewhere in the economy as a result of their exercise of money wage restraint.

Put simply, whether or not the general effects of the introduction of capital sharing schemes will assist the general economic policies of governments depends on whether or not the schemes are effective, i.e. whether they are genuinely accepted by both social partners. If they are not, adverse repercussions can be expected on a number of fronts. If shareholders regard the schemes as an unfair imposition on them there can be a reduction in investment from market-provided funds. Investment funds might flow abroad. Alternatively, they might press managers to restore the previous total return to share-holders, i.e. dividends plus value of retained profits which increase the worth of the equities. (This would lead to price increases which could generate additional wage demands.) If government general demand management policy did not allow some expansion in the economy the increase in prices which was not matched by increases in spendable wages could lead either to unemployment or to a reduction of voluntary savings by workers. The increase in unemployment could adversely affect the other economic aims of government as well as providing undesirable political pressures which could lead to a stimulation of demand in order to restore the previous employ-ment level. Inflation would therefore have occurred which might be greater or less than that which would have occurred without an incomes policy.

Conclusions

Capital-sharing offers some benefit to trade unions in return for restraint in money wage increases. Moreover, it appears to provide one of the few ways of redistributing income and wealth, something which orthodox collective bargaining has not been particularly successful in achieving. The specific attraction of capital sharing is that it redistributes the ownership of wealth assets without leading to an increase in consumption and a reduction in investment resources. (This assumes that workers will not offset their new wealth assets by a reduction in voluntary savings.) In this way, the two goals of a reduction in inflationary pressure and the maintenance or increasing of investment might be reconciled.

Against this, either of the two social partners might not accept the realities of capital sharing. Shareholders might be unwilling to see a redistribution of wealth and workers might continue to try and increase their current real consumption levels at the expense of other income groups. Much depends on the views regarding an acceptable distribution of income, consumption and wealth. If the parties reject the underlying beliefs of capital sharing, there could well be even more adverse economic repercussions than would take place without a scheme.

Possible schemes within an incomes policy

I If incomes policy took the form of a norm for wage increases and similar rules for price increases and decreases, a capital growth-sharing scheme might ease inflationary wage pressure as unions and workers accepted that all profits made by the company would be shared and therefore their wage restraint would not be used to the advantage of other groups. However, with this type of incomes policy there tends to be collusion between the two social partners in any one industry or firm once they have agreed on a wage increase, as they unite against the policy in order to defend the agreement they have reached jointly. There is a danger that this collusion would be even stronger with capital growth-sharing in an incomes policy in that both social partners would have a direct interest in exploiting the consumer through price increases. Normally, if a company increases prices trade unions will seek to take advantage of the resulting higher profits in their wage bargaining, but with capital growth-sharing the gain to employees from higher profits from increasing prices is direct and automatic.

II An alternative approach could be to determine a norm above which no direct spendable wage increases could be given. The two partners would be free to negotiate whatever settlement they wished, but all increases in excess of the norm could be paid only in the form of investment wages, frozen for some pre-determined period of time. (On the prices side, it might be decided that investment wage increases were not counted as "permitted" increases in costs when deciding whether prices should be allowed to rise or whether they should fall.) This proposal has the advantage that it interferes relatively little with the processes of collective bargaining and does not try to impose a settlement which might be contrary to the wishes of both parties. It leaves them free to determine their own increases, but says that only certain parts of them can be paid in cash. On macro-level analysis it might be argued that this will prevent "excessive" wage increases as employers will not be prepared to increase their costs, even supposing they were able to increase prices, as there would not be an equal rise in consumer demand. However, it does not follow that even if this argument is valid at the macro-level it will influence the behaviour of firms at the micro-level. If individual companies or industries believe that they can pass on the higher costs, even though this might lead to a reduction in demand for products of other sectors, they may well do so, with the undesirable inflationary consequences.

Principles for the Creation of a Wage-earners' Profit and Investment Fund

as adopted by the LO's Committee on Economic Democracy on 30th September 1970

Denmark:

(1) A wage-earners' profit and investment fund shall be established by Statute to secure all wage-earners—irrespective of their place of employment—a share in the capital gains of the national economy.

(2) The aims of the fund shall be to contribute towards democratisation of the economy, greater equality in the distribution of property and income and increased savings, and thus to an increased flow of capital to Danish industry and other important sectors of the Danish economy.

(3) The financing of the fund shall be effected through the payment of contributions from all employers—private as well as public—at the rate of 1 per cent of the wage total in respect of the first year of the scheme, increasing yearly by $\frac{1}{2}$ per cent up till 5 per cent.

(4) The amounts paid into the fund by the employers and the annual interest revenues and increments from investments made by the fund shall be the property of the wage-earners. This property right shall be secured for the individual through the issue of personal certificates for equal shares of the total capital of the fund.

(5) Certificates shall be issued in respect of the amounts paid into the fund each year. They shall not be convertible, but the individual holder of certificates shall be able to redeem the certificates in the fund at any time after a freeze period of

five years. Within the five years' period redemption shall, however, be possible if the holder reaches the age of retirement or at the occurrence of death and invalidity.

(6) The fund shall be an independent institution, working in association with the wage-earners' organisations and supervised by the State.

(7) In the case of limited liability companies or co-operative societies the entire contribution shall remain deposited in the enterprise as responsible wage-earners' capital. In other enterprises part of the obligatory payments to the fund may, by arrangement with the fund, remain deposited in the enterprise as responsible wage-earners' capital.

(8) In limited liability companies and co-operative societies the wage-earners' capital shall take the form of shares. In other enterprises the wage-earners' capital shall be placed before the responsible capital of the enterprise, but after all other commitments.

(9) In limited liability companies and co-operative societies the wage-earners' capital shall have a share in the annual profit on an equal footing with other responsible capital and a *pro rata* share in the annual increments from the firm's own capital. In other enterprises interest on wage-earners' capital shall be paid according to the arrangement made with the fund under section 7 above; the fund may stipulate an adjustment of the value of wage-earners' capital in such enterprises. Yield and interest on wage-earners' capital shall annually be paid into the fund.

(10) The wage-earners' capital shall form the basis of the extension of direct democracy in the enterprises in question. In limited liability companies and co-operative societies the wage-earners' capital shall be represented on the board by at least one member and moreover in proportion to the share of the wage-earners' capital in the total capital endowed with voting rights. At the general meeting of a limited liability company or a co-operative society the wage-earners' capital shall be represented by a number of representatives elected by all the employees of the enterprise in commun. Similar rules shall apply to enterprises which are organised as companies of a type other than limited liability companies and co-operative societies. In one-man firms the wage-earners' capital shall be

represented by the wage-earners' representatives in the joint consultation committee (works council).

(11) In connection with the wage-earners' profit and investment fund a special institute shall be established with the task of being at the disposal of the representatives of the wage-earners' capital in analysing the accounts and other financial arrangements of the enterprises.

(12) In the case of liquidation of an enterprise in which wage-earners' capital is deposited the wage-earners' capital in question shall be transferred to the fund.

(13) When a certificate has become redeemable it may at any time be redeemed in the fund at a market value which takes into account average increments since the issue of the certificate and the interest on the total capital of the fund, including wage-earners' capital deposited in enterprises. The aim of this provision is thereby to secure all wage-earners equal capital gains, irrespective of the type of enterprise in which they are employed and irrespective of their employment being public or private.

(14) The part of the resources of the fund which is not deposited in the enterprises as special wage-earners' capital shall preferably be placed through active investment, that is in a way so as to obtain a share in general increments and the highest possible yield. Security shall be obtained through an appropriate dispersal of investments, for instance on shares, real property and bonds.

(15) The fund shall be managed by a council composed of representatives of the various organisations of wage-earners: the LO, the FTF (association of organisations of civil servants and salaried employees) and others, and by a board of five members, four of which shall be elected by the council and one appointed by the State.

(16) In association with the fund shall be established local committees and branch committees with representatives of the enterprises (shop stewards) and of the wage-earners' organisations; their task shall be to advise in matters relating to the placing of the resources of the fund.

Calculations with regard to the size of the fund

With a view to calculating the size of the proposed profit and investment fund it is necessary to establish a number of more or less arbitrary conditions as regards the general economic development in the period after the commencement of the fund.

The following calculations are based on the conditions mentioned below:

1. The total number of wage-earners is supposed to be constant (in terms of workers employed all the year round: 1,750,000).

2. The annual increase in wages is estimated at permanently 8 per cent, the wage total at permanently 50 per cent of the gross national product (wage total in 1970 approximately 63 milliard Dkr.).

3. The capital of the fund is estimated to increase by 8 per cent per year as a consequence of interest and increments.

4. Administrative expenses are not taken into consideration because, in all circumstances, they will soon constitute an insignificant part of the total fund.

5. It is estimated that the market value of the total share capital and co-operative capital in the Danish economy in 1970 is approximately 30 milliard Dkr. and that this value will increase annually by 10 per cent as a consequence of appropriations, new subscription of responsible capital (including wage-earners' capital), etc.

6. It is estimated that increments on the companies' own capital will be 3 per cent per year, and that the average profit per year will be 5 per cent of the total value of own capital.

7. Wage-earners' capital in the companies is only foreseen in cases where it is obligatory, and it is supposed that 30 per cent of total wages emanate from the companies, and that consequently also 30 per cent of the annual contribution will each year remain in the companies as newly subscribed wage-earners' capital.

8. The payment of assets from the fund which will follow from the access to full redemption at the reaching of retirement age and at the occurrence of invalidity etc. has not been taken into consideration. On the other hand it has been foreseen that everybody will draw his money immediately when the certificate will normally become redeemable. As it is to be expected

that the fund will be an attractive form of savings it may also be safe to expect that an increasing part of convertible shares will not be converted immediately and that, in the period after the convertibility is beginning to make itself felt, the working capital of the fund will therefore be considerably higher than supposed in the foregoing.

Total capital of the fund (in Dkr.)

After five years from the start of the scheme the total capital of the fund will be well over 9 milliards, after 10 years just under 30 milliards.

The share of the total capital of the scheme in the gross national product

After five years from the start the fund will have reached an amount corresponding to 5 per cent of the gross national product, after 10 years corresponding to 11 per cent, and from the 14th year (when, under the given conditions, there will be equilibrium between in- and outgoing payments) the fund will stabilise at a permanent share of $12\frac{1}{2}$ per cent, which means that the fund will grow pari passu with total incomes.

The share of wage-earners' capital in total capital assets

During the first 5 years, when no payments will be made to the wage-earners, the wage-earners' capital will constitute a slightly declining share of the total capital assets, whereas, after that period, the share will be heavily increasing: after 10 years from the start 39 per cent, after 15 years from the start 54 per cent, and after 20 years from the start well over 70 per cent of the total amount of capital assets.

The share of wage-earners' capital in the total responsible capital of the companies

The growth of wage-earners' capital—in relation to the individual company's own capital—will be highly differing. Taken together they will, however, constitute a strongly increasing share of the total responsible capital of the companies: after 5 years about 5 per cent, after 10 years about 14 per cent, after 15 years about 21 per cent, and after 20 years about 26 per cent. It will be seen that the rate of increase in the wage-earners' capital will gradually become weaker, but that the wage-earners will comparatively soon attain a fairly strong position as shareholders.

Addendum

In January 1973 the LO and the Socialist Party in Denmark reached agreement on proposed legislation to be introduced to establish a capital-sharing scheme. This followed the outlines of the LO's 1970 scheme with some modifications. The most important was that the employers' contribution to the Fund should be based on two criteria: a percentage of the wage bill as originally suggested, and also a percentage of profits which might be of the equivalent order of 5 per cent of the wage bill. No company would be required to deposit more than the equivalent of 50 per cent of its shares in the Fund. Once this limit has been reached, further contributions would be in cash. The Fund could, however, purchase shares on the open market so that its holdings of the shares of a particular company could exceed 50 per cent. The effect of these two amendments is to increase the possible contribution of companies, in some cases, on certain assumptions, from an ultimate figure of 5 per cent of the wage bill to something like 10 per cent of the wage bill. In addition, if companies pay in cash after shares equal to 50 per cent of the equity have been passed to the Fund, the price effects of the scheme might be different from those originally envisaged. There may be greater pressure for price increases to recover the cash payments. At the time of writing, however, the final details are not available, nor is it known whether the proposed legislation will, in fact, pass through the legislature.

CHAPTER 6

Trade Unions and Multinational Companies

The growth of multinational companies has numerous important consequences not only for trade unions but for governments, employers' associations, international organisations and those trying to produce economic theories which help explain the events of the real world. These companies pose questions which might necessitate the complete reassessment of the traditional theory of international trade between countries. They may challenge the hitherto normally accepted view that governments have both the right and the ability to levy taxation on those activities taking place within their national boundaries. They make it extremely difficult, if not impossible, for any single government to know just what activities are taking place within that country and what amounts of profits are properly ascribable to these activities. The ability of large multinational companies to take their profit where it best suits them and to switch large sums of internal funds from country to country, or simply to delay or speed up the transmission of funds by leads and lags, can have serious repercussions on a country's balance of payments and effectively limit a government's powers to deal with an adverse balance in the easiest and most effective way. Traditional views that there exists a common sense of purpose within a country, or that there is some "national interest" which should be advanced, are challenged by the growth of companies operating in a number of countries and which probably have their headquarters in some foreign country. It is thought that it is much more difficult to influence the location and type of investment and employment opportunities within a country if the ultimate decision-taking authority of companies is located overseas. Trade unions are aware of the problems stemming from an inability to come to grips with effective decision-takers. Although the seminar was primarily interested in trade union problems and looked at the issues firstly from a trade union viewpoint, those taking part were nevertheless conscious of the broader issues and of the need for governments and other organisations to consider the changed circumstances resulting from the growth of multi-national companies.

Many of the problems discussed were not new. For example trade unions have long had to deal with multi-plant national companies where the location of effective authority was blurred or, possibly deliberately, hidden or confused. Threats to move the location of the plant to another part of the country where wages might be lower and trade union organisation non-existent have been made for a very long time and did not need multinational companies to invent them. What this new type of company has done, however, is to magnify the problem and change its nature by removing it to the international level cutting across national boundaries, institutions and loyalties. This is why there is need for such seminars as this one.

I Definitions

There is no single definition of a multinational company which is widely accepted. The various approaches to the question of definition are of two main types: (1) those that seek to adopt some criteria of a quantifiable nature, e.g. companies which own producing facilities or subsidiaries in more than a given number of countries, or which have a stated proportion of their assets, sales or earnings overseas, (2) those definitions which, while adopting some minimum qualification regarding overseas activities, base the crucial qualification on the company's behaviour or attitude. This might refer to the internal management organisation structure and the relative importance of different forms of operations or might be based on the psychological attitudes of managers along lines produced by Perlmutter, ethnocentric-home country oriented; polycentric-host country oriented; geocentric-world oriented.

It was generally agreed that no single definition would satisfy all purposes, but the most important feature common to multinational companies from a trade union point of view was that these companies had *power centres* outside the country in which the establishments concerned were operating. This means that trade unions and governments outside the country in which the company's home is based do not have the same influence, or the opportunity to exert the same influence, as they do with nationally based companies. It may also be that the government and unions in the home country found their freedom of action reduced relatively by a large multinational company, particularly if the home country is small.

Many economists producing a definition or guide along these lines would probably refer to "decision-taking centres" rather than power centres. The choice of terminology by the seminar emphasises the primary nature of trade union concern with this question. Trade unions are bargaining institutions; they exist in order to bargain and exert influence on behalf of their members, although they have other wider objectives and may see their members' interests in a very broad framework. They recognise, perhaps much more readily and clearly than some other observers, the importance of the location of power as it affects decision-taking and the ability of other bodies, be they unions, governments or international agencies, to influence the decision-takers. Power is particularly important in relation to decision to locate investment and production in different places, with the obvious effects on both the terms and conditions and level of employment. Because of this emphasis the group was less concerned to include within the definition such overseas activity as a selling agency. The emphasis was on production subsidiaries, which could include retail outlets where the actual stores were owned by the multinational company. In some cases it might also be desirable to include companies which, while not operating in a number of countries, were producing in some country other than their "normal" home, such as the foot-loose companies constantly moving in search of cheap labour but which had management and ownership based on one country. From a trade union viewpoint, some of the problems involved with this sort of company are similar to those with a manufacturing company operating in a number of countries. Basically, therefore, the group wished to discuss the problems arising from the existence of a large, and growing number of companies which operate in overseas countries but excluding those that have merely a sales office or some equivalent small organisation abroad.

II Types of multinational companies

The distinctions brought out by Professor Perlmutter were regarded as providing a useful classification scheme and illustrating the three stages through which a company might move, although not everyone was convinced that this pattern of development was general in application. Thus, as well as giving a means of distinguishing companies into three types, Perlmutter implies that the company will progress through three stages of development of policy and attitudes, each represented by a classification.

Companies often start by being *ethnocentric* with policies determined, or heavily influenced, by conditions, customs and conventions of the home country. Although there is little reliable and detailed evidence available, the impression is that American companies operating abroad may have stronger tendencies towards ethnocentric policies than do companies from other countries. This is often demonstrated most sharply in questions affecting trade union recognition and bargaining rights, and particularly where the company does not recognise or bargain with trade unions at home, or does not do so for certain grades, e.g. white collar or executive/technical employees. Often foreign companies have had difficulties too, e.g. the tendency for quite high grade executives in France to join "cadres" with trade union implications.

It is possible that in the case of American companies some of the features noted as ethnocentric behaviour might be manifestations of normal management practice by American companies who generally exercise a greater degree of centralised control over subsidiaries, both foreign and domestic, in various parts of the United States, than do European countries. It may be that superimposed on the patterns of ethnocentric behaviour are organisational characteristics reflecting centralised or decentralised management structures, which are the result of basic managerial policy essentially unconnected with the overseas aspects of the companies' activities. However, it was generally believed that in addition to this there was a tendency for companies in the early part of their overseas activities to adopt policies, techniques, behavioural and cultural patterns based on, if not determined by, their home experience.

6

The second stage is that of *polycentric* policies and attitudes. Here, the company becomes oriented towards the host country and adopts behaviour patterns more in keeping with practices in that country, and may go so far as to identify itself primarily with the host rather than the parent country.

It was generally thought that the third stage, the *geocentric* company, which is world-oriented and therefore presumably biassed neither towards its "parent" country nor its host countries, has not yet emerged, although a very few companies such as Shell or Unilever are really neither ethnocentric nor polycentric. They may be in a stage where they adopt neutral types of policy in that they are biased towards neither of the major countries in which their shareholders live, nor unduly towards the particular country in which a particular establishment is operating, but they have not yet moved to the stage where their policies can be described as truly world-oriented. It might be that the last stage of development will be towards a limited geocentricity covering only those countries in which the company actually operates rather than the whole world. The third stage is still something of an unknown quantity and might well need to be reassessed in the light of actual developments.

It was believed that there is no single unique pattern of development followed by all firms. Nevertheless certain trends were observed. When companies first operate abroad they tend to take with them industrial relations behaviour based on experience and practice in their home country. This is the experience best known by management and is the kind of practice with which they have often been brought up. This feature is particularly marked in the case of companies starting operations in developing countries. The company may have a philosophy of its own, e.g. a marked preference for a certain kind of payment system, or a particularly individualistic approach to profit-sharing or employee participation, or it may just have a broad attitude to industrial relations as practised at home. Parent companies often adopt different attitudes to qualitative changes than to quantitative changes proposed by subsidiaries, as the former might include issues of principle.

Policies based on home practices tend to run into difficulties sooner or later, as pressures build up in the host country for industrial relations policies more in keeping with the general patterns in that country. The imposition of foreign traditions can be a constant source of potential conflict, pressures for change to conform with general patterns of behaviour will be constantly exerted. Companies may then adapt to the new environment, to bring practices more into line with those existing in the rest of the country. The speed with which they can adapt in this way may be influenced by the relative importance of the foreign activity to the parent company. It was suggested that in this respect American firms differ from, say, Swedish firms in that with the former the overseas activities are seldom more than a small part of total activity, while for the latter companies they may form the great majority of the companies' business so that they are particularly concerned to avoid any major industrial difficulties which might jeopardise production and total profits. Adaptation to the conditions in the host country can be expected to be considerably quicker in these cases.

After some experience of this stage the larger companies operating in a number of countries may well run into further difficulties. The problem of co-ordination becomes increasingly more complex; polycentric policies often place much greater emphasis on adaptation to the needs and conditions of the host country as a whole than to the needs of the company as a whole. The company may then seek to develop different policies based on a geocentric approach which permit it to co-ordinate commercial policies to some extent by formulating a super-national industrial relations policy which is not primarily determined by the needs of either the "home" country or of the individual host country in which a particular establishment happens to be located, e.g. Shell. The company and its needs on an international level become more important than the traditions and behaviour patterns of any one country, even the country of origin.

Multinational companies may prove to be ethnocentric in some respects, polycentric in others and geocentric in yet others.

III The Location of Power in Multinational Companies

Consideration of the stages through which a multinational company may pass necessarily includes some discussion of the location of power within the company. Indeed to some extent the demarcation of the various stages is based on the transfer of power from one country to another within the whole organisation, but it is also influenced by the type of decisions taken at various power centres. The distinction between ethnocentric and polycentric companies is not the same as that between companies with centralised and decentralised decision-taking. It is possible that decision-taking is decentralised so that each subsidiary of the company is free structurally and organisationally to take such decision as it chooses and yet the decisions that are taken are essentially ethnocentric in character. The values and standards of the parent company can be inculcated into the national subsidiaries so that the type and quality of policy decisions are exactly the same as they would be were they to be taken by the company headquarters in the home country. Or the cross-pressures can work the other way. Some American companies operating in Latin America have introduced a policy of replacing United States personnel in the higher-ranking posts with nationals of the country concerned, and have had to insist on the acceptance of this policy in the face of opposition from the local subsidiaries. The subsidiaries were managed by American personnel who no doubt believed their own personal interests might be threatened, but nevertheless if the company had created a decentralised framework of decision-taking, the American personnel would have remained in positions of authority so that the policies of the subsidiaries would probably have been much more American-oriented—or ethnocentric—than would be the case when nationals of the home country were appointed to positions of authority. It need not follow therefore that centralisation of some decisions within a company need necessarily imply an overwhelming ethnocentric policy.

In developing countries companies may turn out to be bad employers even though they are not so regarded at home. Often this is because the company has no centralised industrial relations policy and the executives dealing with these questions overseas are not personnel specialists. In these cases the production or marketing executives take on some responsibilities for industrial relations often reluctantly—and adopt the less advanced standards and norms of the home country.

Thus it does not follow that because policies are ethnocentric they have been imposed from the home country. It may be a sign of the lack of attention given to industrial relations that the local management, and often the top posts tend to be filled by nationals from the home country, who adopt policies based on their experience and hazy knowledge of practices in the home country. Or it may be that companies "export" certain practices but not all. For example American companies might be more likely to try and introduce their lay-off procedures in Europe than their grievance procedures. When criticism is made of the practice of importing foreign industrial relations practices it may be that the criticism is based on the unwelcome parts of the foreign practice only.

In summary it can be said that power can be located either in the home or the host country and that while this is often the crucial question which determines the types of policies which the company is likely to follow, it can happen that the extent of centralisation and the degree of ethnocentricity are not the same.

Types of power centres

There are a number of different possible locations of power. The location of power for industrial relations purposes is a combination of two factors. Firstly, there is the straightforward power or ability to negotiate terms and conditions of employment in an orthodox collective bargaining sense, so that subsidiaries might have autonomy to recognise unions and bargain with them or they might only have the ability to act as agents of headquarters. Secondly, there is the power to take other decisions, which are not necessarily regarded by management as industrial relations questions, but which have both direct and significant impact on industrial relations, e.g. investment and output decisions.

Industrial relations decisions

Trade unions believe that they are often misled as companies conceal the real location of effective power. In some situations, local management may say that they would like to concede a trade union demand but do not have the power to do so. In other cases they may pretend to have the power but refuse to exercise it in order to escape the criticism that they are "foreign-dominated". There is often a suspicion by employees that their local management does not have the autonomy necessary to participate in effective collective bargaining and that in certain key areas the parent company takes the basic decision. Similar problems may be found in bargaining with a multi-plant company which operates entirely within the domestic boundaries, but in this case it is possible, although perhaps difficult, for trade unions to enter into a bargaining relationship with both the local plant and the headquarters, and the various possible locations are all, in principle, within the area of bargaining by the national trade unions. This is not the case with multinational companies.

Company policy may change through time and the growth of polycentric attitudes may bring the location of industrial relations policy within the national boundary. Often this change of policy will be actively encouraged by the trade unions. Again differences were noted between operations in developed and developing countries. Companies were also differentiated in developed countries according to whether they had been founded by the foreign parent company setting up a new enterprise, whether a previously nationally-owned company had been taken over, or whether a joint enterprise, with both foreign and national ownership, had been formed. The influence of foreign industrial relations practices was greater in the first kind of situation.

In some cases the location of power to take industrial relations decisions is determined by general company policy of centralisation which makes little distinction between either domestic or overseas subsidiaries. The company may have developed a policy on such things as trade union recognition which is applied equally in all its plants no matter where they are located, subject only to any legal restraints imposed in particular countries.

Economic decisions

The second type of power is often regarded as more difficult to deal with. This is because to some extent it is hidden; companies do not normally publicise the processes by which they take investment or output decisions, nor do they usually publicise the content of those decisions in advance of their implementation. The competitive pressures of industry and possibly anti-trust regulations governing information agreements etc. might be sufficient to cause this. To trade unionists these decisions can be the most important ones. These decisions can affect the level of employment. Jobs can be taken away instantly by decisions to switch production from one country to another or to invest in one country rather than another. Moreover, the threat to switch investment and even to close down existing plants is sometimes made during negotiations in an attempt to induce unions to moderate their demands. While it was thought that investment decisions probably have been altered as a result of trade union demands, or labour conditions, in particular countries, there was no evidence that companies had actually closed down plants and transferred the activity to some other country. (This excludes switching of production during the course of an industrial dispute which will be discussed below.)

The centralisation of investment decisions is almost a universal feature of multinational companies. Multinational companies are often formed in order to take advantage of returns to scale in investment, marketing or technological areas. It would be unusual if the central organisation made no attempt at all to co-ordinate the activities of the various subsidiaries. There will therefore be considerable centralisation of these economic decisions. There are some signs that the centralisation is increasing as firms seek to specialise and integrate production in different countries.

The question of the location of economic power is a crucial one for trade unionists. The ability to switch economic resources from country to country, or to threaten to, is a powerful weapon which can be used to considerable effect by a company. When this power is associated with a desire (by governments) to increase the industrialisation or modernisation of industry and increase employment, the ability of companies to allocate economic resources on an international level is reinforced by the competing national aspirations and policies of the various labour forces or trade union movements. There is a possibility that a form of competitive underbidding among various national workforces will develop as a company "plays off" one country against another. Trade unions have traditionally held it to be one of their prime functions to prevent the competitive cutting of standards by individual workers and they are now beginning to explore the possibility of co-ordinated action on an international scale, to prevent any development of competitive cutting by individual national movements. However, it is not only trade unions who should be concerned in this respect. Governments too can be subjected to the same pressures as they seek to attract additional investment, particularly when they are seeking to develop those areas with higher than average unemployment or to attract companies with superior technological skills. The effects of the exercise of their special powers by multinational companies can extend beyond what are normally regarded as "trade union issues". Regional economic organisations might serve as countervailing forces to multinational companies by creating more standard conditions within the areas.

We will first consider the effect on industrial relations and conditions of employment and then the broader economic questions.

Acceptance of the right to organise and bargain collectively

Collective bargaining has developed in different ways in different countries, and is at different stages of development. Some of the difficulties ascribed to dealing with multinational companies in a particular country may reflect the specific conditions of that country rather than problems of multinational companies as such. Thus in some cases when there are difficulties regarding the establishment of effective bargaining rights at factory level, this might also be true of many national companies.

Companies often behave differently in different countries. Some will recognise unions in Europe but not in developing countries. This is particularly true of some American companies which recognise unions in the United States but will pay higher wages than they might otherwise have to do in South America in order to keep out trade unions which they regard as politically motivated, and in this sense not "true" trade unions.

It was thought that, on the whole, there were no major areas of difficulty with European companies operating elsewhere in Europe, although this might not be true of their activities in developing countries. By and large these companies tend to adopt the general attitudes and behaviour of the host country. On the other hand, there was a feeling that American companies tended to wait until they were pressed and the union had demonstrated its strength and membership before granting recognition. To some extent this was probably a reflection of American practice where recognition is not automatic and unions have first to win it.

There was no desire to seek to compel incoming multinational companies to recognise trade unions. This demonstrates the deep-rooted objection of trade unions to bring the government into the field of collective bargaining. However, interest was expressed in the Swedish practice whereby when the government guarantees the investment of Swedish firms operating abroad, one of the conditions is that the firm should follow the best trade union relations in the host country. Presumably this degree of government intervention is acceptable because it operates only against the company and in respect to its activities in another country. This form of exerting pressure has one great advantage; it is the strong country which imposes the conditions. The receiving countries are often economically weak and anxious to have the incoming investment and so are in a disadvantageous position to seek to impose conditions, particularly if they try to do so in isolation.

Wage policy
This has two aspects, (1) wage or payment systems, and (2) the wage level.

Wage systems
Generally a company has a common philosophy on wage payment systems. This tends to be as true of multiplant

6*

national companies as of multinational companies. Moreover, as the wage system becomes increasingly determined by the technology of the industry concerned it is likely that uniform payment systems will spread through an industry irrespective of the individual company concerned and in large part irrespective of the country in which the operations take place. Individual companies may have their own company-based additions such as profit-sharing for white collar employees or staff status for blue-collar workers, and these will probably continue to be exported to the various countries of operation.

It is possible that multinational companies may have a little more freedom to adopt a completely different wage system when setting up a new plant. As they are newcomers they may not be subject to the same degree of pressure to follow the existing pattern. Moreover as the incidence of payment-by-results tends to be less in the United States than elsewhere, it is probable that American companies abroad will adopt time-based payment systems even though the domestic sector of the industry does not, e.g. the auto industry in England.

Wage levels

There was a general consensus that, in developing countries, multinational companies tended to pay higher wages than domestic ones, but this could be due to the type of industry. There was no such general opinion in respect of multinational companies in Europe. However, comparisons are extremely difficult; there are few data available and such figures as there are, are complicated by the fact that multinational companies tend to be large and earnings are correlated with size of plant. Moreover it is not clear whether the appropriate comparison should be with firms in the same industry or in the same locality. It was thought that some multinational companies pay higher than corresponding domestic ones and some pay less. In some cases, evidence was available to show that a single multinational company had a number of disparate wage levels within the same country, some high and some relatively low, e.g. International Harvester in France. Often executives may be paid relatively highly. This may be necessary in order to attract new staff, or because the need to have internationally mobile executives, or compensate the nationals of the home country who may occupy the senior positions, leads to higher salary levels than domestically-based and single country companies.

If the multinational company is using much more advanced and developed machinery and techniques, wages may be higher, but if this is payment for higher-skilled labour, a straight comparison is misleading. Similarly if the company is deliberately paying higher wages to keep trade unions out, the more appropriate comparison would be with similarly placed domestic companies which were trying to buy freedom from trade unions and not with the generality of domestic companies.

Membership of employers' associations

In some cases multinational companies, especially American-owned ones, are reluctant to join employers' associations, while in others they appear to join to the same extent as domestic firms. In the first case it is possible that the reluctance stems from the full obligations of membership. For example, in Britain the company may be required to follow a certain procedure for settling disputes which could in the last resort require the company to accept a decision taken by either a joint employer-trade union body, or by a committee of fellow-employers. Companies may not be prepared to accept this. Similarly if the collective agreement could require that the wage level be uniformly and precisely adopted, so that there are no company additions, many firms may be unwilling to surrender this degree of freedom of action.

On the other hand where the agreed wage is only a minimum so that firms are free to pay above it should they wish, multinational companies may have no reservations about joining the association. This is probably why these companies join them in Italy, for example, where the larger companies, domestic as well as multinational, pay in excess of the collectively agreed regional wage. These companies are thus able to exert some degree of collective control over the minimum increase in wages of other firms and to claim that they participate in bargaining with trade unions, while at the same time they retain effective control over the wage level in their own hands. This has the additional advantage to them that the "trade union rate" is seen to be less than the rate actually paid by the company and so acts as a disincentive to union membership. Companies may bargain with trade unions at regional or national level but oppose strenuously any union attempt to bargain at plant level.

Fringe Benefits

It seems to be generally agreed that multinational companies often provide better fringe benefits than domestic companies, and this is particularly so in developing countries. In a number of these there may be legal requirements to provide a minimum —often a fairly high minimum—level of various benefits but these may not be observed in practice. There is a much stronger tendency for the managerial philosophy of companies to repeat itself in fringe benefits than in, say, wage patterns, as fringes often illustrate some basic aspect of that philosophy to a much greater degree. It is usual to find a uniform comprehensive personnel policy which draws together various benefits in a coherent whole.

Ability of firms to shift investment and employment opportunities

It is not only multinational companies who have the power to move their production to other countries. For example, some Swedish firms have moved to Portugal to take advantage of lower wages. Also some governments try to attract incoming foreign investment and production to increase domestic employment levels, particularly in areas of higher unemployment, and to obtain the benefits of superior technology or know-how. Thus it is not just that companies have the ability to move, they may be subject to strong inducement by governments to do so. In other cases the important issue may be the supply of labour, so that the question facing the company and the domestic government is whether it is preferable for the firm to move elsewhere or for foreign workers to be attracted to the country to provide the necessary labour.

The ability of firms to change their location is determined to some extent by technological or geographical factors. Not all companies are able to move. They may do so only at very high cost, or may have only few other possible locations. From a profit viewpoint it may be that the location of the distribution centres is much more important than the location of production.

If trading companies can be established in countries of low taxation, internal book-keeping may allow profit to be maximised to a greater extent than would result from transferring productive facilities without an international distribution company. Wage or labour cost differences might be heavily outweighed by tax considerations, and once investment has taken place there is little danger of it moving. Companies may divert future investment and production, depending on the production-flows and technological features, but they very rarely completely close down existing plants and transfer the whole operations elsewhere. The main exceptions are the footloose "run-away" companies which typically operate in such fields as textiles or light electronic assembly and induce governments to offer considerable concessions. Once costs rise at all, the company moves elsewhere in pursuit of similar concessions and high profits.

Companies establish themselves overseas for various reasons:

(a) to obtain access to a foreign market;
(b) to reduce transport costs to their overseas markets;
(c) to produce more cheaply and export back to the mother country, thus becoming competitive again.

The particular reasons for the company moving abroad initially will be relevant to its threats to again change its location in the face of trade union pressure for improved wages and working conditions.

It does seem clear that in some cases companies divert production to cheaper locations, just as they do within the various plants of a multiplant national company, both private and state-owned. This shift of production is much more likely to occur during a trade dispute. The International Trade Union Federations are aware of this and try to take appropriate action to stop it.

However, ultimately, questions of the location of investment and employment, the tax or other concessions to be offered to firms to come in to an area, the consequences of their leaving if presented with higher wage demands or increased labour costs, are questions about government economic policy and are not something which can be settled by trade unions and management participating in bilateral collective bargaining.

At the end of the day government has to be brought into the discussion and trade unions will need to concern themselves with economic decision-taking.

Trade Union Response

(a) *Local level*

Workers involved in a take-over by a multinational company very often feel themselves to be in a conflict situation. In many cases the company has been taken over because it is less efficient or profitable than its competitors and the incoming owners are probably bringing new techniques, more efficient production methods and a determination to improve the profitability of the firm. There may be early conflicts over non-wage issues such as streamlining of production, manning scales, the re-allocation of labour, redundancy etc. Problems may be particularly acute in countries which have statutory protection of jobs so that redundancy is normally much less frequent than in the company's mother country, so that the actions of the multinational company are correspondingly felt to be even more objectionable.

An example of trade union demands following the take-over of a domestic company by a foreign firm are:

(1) the level of employment is to be safeguarded;

(2) guarantees regarding job and income security in the event of downgrading to be given;

(3) there should be no displacement of research;

(4) national management should continue and not be replaced by international management;

(5) the state should become a shareholder;

(6) there should be an agreement to safeguard conditions during the transfer of ownership and there should be no switch of production without trade union consultation;

(7) there should be stronger trade union representation in the factory and contact should be established with trade unions in the company's mother country.

Some of these demands came from the national level of the trade union and some from the plant level. Not all of them were met, but they illustrate the sort of safeguards trade unions might seek to obtain.

(b) *National level*

In Britain the TUC point out that the activities of British international companies are in broad terms as important (e.g. in terms of total exports from Britain to related companies overseas) as the activities of foreign-owned international companies. The TUC argues that the Government has strong interest therefore in the results of both outward and inward investment. The Government's scrutiny of proposals for new inward investment is therefore seen as part of a balanced assessment of the relation of both inward and outward investment to the balance of payments and employment and economic development generally. A resolution adopted by the 1969 Congress drew attention to the transformation of major British companies into multinational corporations which, if not controlled by the extension of social ownership and/or a system of public accountability, would create new problems of job security and economic difficulties.

The Canadian Trade Union Congress recently called for the publication of details about foreign firms in Canada, including financial details. Canada probably has more foreign-owned companies operating within its boundaries and controlling a larger part of her economy than any other developed country. At the other extreme it might be argued that the national trade union movement can do little but seek to ensure that the individual companies are fully organised by the appropriate trade unions and that normal collective bargaining processes are used to obtain satisfactory agreements on those subjects of importance to workers.

The point at which there was most agreement was that the national trade unions should urge government to try and secure some international code of good conduct for multinational companies.

(c) *International level*

While international collective bargaining might be an attractive ideal for which to work, it is not a practical proposition in the foreseeable future. The next stage of development is likely to

be international support for national bargaining, although the
national bargaining itself might be co-ordinated to some extent.
Initially it is probable that co-ordination will take place
between the various national branches of a single large multinational company rather than for a full industry, but to begin
with it is unlikely to cover more than a few countries. It is not
thought that there will be uniform demands; different countries may press for different amounts of wage increases, but
they may try to synchronise the timing of the claims and
terminal dates of contracts and may submit similar demands
on non-wage issues, such as training, trade union rights, access
to information and details of future plans etc. Thus it is likely
that there will be international organisation at company level
before there is effective action at international trade union
level, and the International Federations will play a part in
co-ordinating or organising the company structures. Action
might then be concentrated in a World Council for the firm,
e.g. Fords or General Motors.

Efforts to date have concentrated more on the pooling of
information through International Federations and the occas-
ional use of trade union strength in those countries where it is
greatest, to exert pressure on behalf of less well developed
organisations. This has been used to transfer on the international level trade union strength in times of dispute. There
will probably be a growth of agreement within companies not
to increase output in any country if there is a dispute at any
plant. In some cases this had already gone to the extent of
banning all overtime in all plants in the event of a dispute
anywhere. It is not always possible to commit all plants in this
way; in some countries there is no effective free movement.

There are difficulties in the way of further trade union co-
operation. The practice of company bargaining is uneven in
incidence. If the system is one of national bargaining, the
international co-ordination necessary may not be possible. It is
doubtful if the Swedish unions could participate in such co-
ordinated bargaining with a large multinational company. On
the other hand it may be possible for unions to have a clause
in their agreements which allows them to strike on solidarity
grounds even though they might not be able to do so for
internal or "selfish" reasons. That the trade union movement

is discussing such possibilities is a measure of the degree of international aid which is possible and is, incidentally, a reason why analyses of unions in purely economic terms fail to understand the vein of moral principle and commitment running through trade union action.

While there may be many difficulties in the way of international collective bargaining and while even co-ordinated national bargaining may run into a number of obstacles there should be no doubt as to the view of many sections of the international trade union movement of the desirability of this as an ultimate goal. It may be that progress towards this will be slow and uneven in incidence between different sectors and industries, but there is a deep-rooted attraction which stems not only from the basic international principles of trade unionism but also from an actue awareness of the necessity of such progress if the realities of economic life as represented by the growth of multinational companies are to be faced. To this end trade unions may use the existing trade union organisations, particularly the industrial organisations, or they may develop new forms of organisations for international co-operation.

An alternative way of exerting pressure is to attack the company's image. In some countries a consumer boycott of the product could be effective. In other countries such a boycott would be against the law. Trade unions can only educate their members not to buy the products.

As the question of workers' participation in management becomes more important, there will be special problems associated with multinational companies. All the questions of the location of power will emerge in an acute form. For example, should trade unionists from other countries be entitled to sit on the main boards in the parent countries? If that is where power is located ought that not to be where the international trade union representation is felt? There are some developments along these lines, e.g. the International Canning Corporation each year holds a conference with trade unions at which it gives advance notice of investment plans and so on and German trade unionists have now been invited by the American Steelworkers Union to attend and ask questions; Philips meet with representatives of trade unions from the six

EEC countries and have agreed to inform them of investment plans and will also inform the International Metalworkers Federation of plans which affect other countries.

Special problems arise from the ability of multinational companies to transfer their profit within the company. Already there is some evidence that unions might seek to bargain on the basis of the consolidated accounts rather than on the accounts for their own country. Thus even though no profit is shown in one particular country the unions may still press for a wage increase on the grounds of general ability to pay. There will probably be a growth of co-operation with trade union centres in the mother country providing detailed information from the central accounts. This development does not reduce the need for accurate and reliable accounts on a national basis. These are especially important where a company is threatening to close down particular plants.

It is necessary to recognise that there are also conflicts between national trade unions. Workers in more developed countries sometimes regard the operation of multinational companies as a threat to their jobs and incomes. They believe their current employment may be jeopardised by cheaper labour overseas, although they are also conscious of the fact that low wage labour is not necessarily cheap labour; workers are as aware of the distinction between wages and unit labour costs as are managements. In some cases workers will be so anxious to attract investment which will provide employment opportunities that they may allow accepted trade union standards to go. In the longer run this sort of situation can lead to hostility against the incoming company; when workers are used to having jobs they frequently resent the fact that in their desperation for work they were obliged to accept standards below those regarded as minimally satisfactory.

The various trade union movements will continue to discuss ways in which they can increase co-operation to their mutual advantage. They are aware of the possible conflicts of interests and so can seek to minimise them. Their approach, based on either the International Federations or specially created company-structured organisations, is increasingly tempered by a realistic appreciation of the nature of the problems and the possible opportunities for co-operation.

Trade unions are concerned to prevent the flight of investment and production which is merely seeking to escape the established provisions for the protection of workers' standards. When companies do this inside a country it is possible to insist that they will observe certain minima. Flight overseas prevents this and could lead to harmful effects on the workers of the mother country. One way to prevent this would be to impose restrictions on the outflow of funds but not to the extent that this hindered the industrialisation of developing countries. The conditions ought not therefore to be merely restrictive; they should have positive features which would allow them to be applied in such a way that the end results were beneficial to both countries.

The importance of subjects not traditionally seen as being of direct concern to trade unions is emphasised. Unions now recognise only too well the importance and relevance of such things as accounting procedures, capital flows, import and export developments and so on. Further, without the stimulus of external pressures, governments may be reluctant to tackle these problems.

The Role of Governments

There was some disagreement over the role governments ought to adopt. Some believe that governments should impose restrictions on both outgoing and incoming capital to ensure that certain minimum standards are maintained in the receiving country. Others believe that receiving countries are in too weak a position to try and impose conditions and that it should be left to the parent countries to ensure that multinational companies do not abuse their relatively strong bargaining position. Others do not favour any restrictions on these companies but would like governments to reach agreement between themselves.

It is generally recognised that some government intervention is necessary. Helpful though international organisations can be, they cannot themselves provide conditions in which collective bargaining can take place, and all trade unions are deeply committed to the principle of collective bargaining as a means of determining terms and conditions of employment.

It is important that there be a common approach by governments if the companies are to be prevented from playing-off one government against another. Even so, the economic position of the country has to be borne in mind. It is unrealistic to expect that all governments will have a common identity of purpose. Some will be much more eager to attract new investment than others and therefore might not co-operate so readily. Similarly, governments in strong positions will be reluctant to impose restrictions on "their" companies if the result is that companies from some other country undertake the investment instead. Countries do have common interests but they also have conflicting interests in specific situations, and there will be differences of view between host and mother countries.

In some cases there will be more direct conflict. For example, a government might wish to insist that an incoming company undertakes research in order to strengthen research in that country as a whole, but the parent company might find it expensive to duplicate research; indeed the overseas venture might be profitable only because it is possible to spread the parent country research expenditure and results over larger outputs, but not worthwhile otherwise.

Provided that governments recognise that they have some conflicts of interests as well as common interests, it is possible to obtain agreement on some features so that incoming companies would be required to observe certain minimum conditions. It is thought that these agreements can best be reached through the medium of international organisations such as the OECD, ILO and World Bank. If concerted action was taken to ensure that, for example, incoming investment, while adopting advanced techniques, did not necessarily adopt the same capital/labour ratios in developing countries as in developed countries with labour shortages, it would be possible to reduce the apprehensions of workers in the advanced countries while helping those in the developing countries. In all cases, even in those countries wishing to impose restrictions on the outflow of capital, it was stressed that this should not be done in a way which would lead to hardship in developing countries. There is a deep and genuine desire to aid developing countries. Moreover, competitive bidding to attract foreign capital is no more justifiable than competitive undercutting of exchange rates.

Governments should ascertain many more facts about the

extent and nature of the operation of multinational companies. The ability to transfer profits, to delay or speed up payments into or out of the country, the size of the capital outflows and the resulting patterns of international trade can all have serious consequences on a country's balance of payments. If special concessions are offered to foreign companies to attract them, or if they enter primarily to gain the advantages of trading areas or customs unions, it is possible for the industrial structure and certainly the foreign trade structure to become seriously distorted with serious consequences on the economy. It is possible that governments distinguish two aspects of the problem. Firstly, there is the act of investment and the opportunity to impose conditions on the incoming company. In large part this is an international problem, but if the company is taking over an existing concern it is possible that there is a margin of opportunity for the government to seek certain conditions. Secondly, there is the continuing survey of activities of multinational companies in all their aspects.

Alternatively, some proposals would affect all large companies. They would be investigated and their pricing and investment practices examined. They might have to report annually to their workers, or the government could appoint public directors. The accounting practices could be studied. Governments would find this difficult to do for multinational companies, and perhaps some international organisation such as the OECD, EEC or EFTA could undertake the study or even impose an international tax.

The actions of multinational companies can compel governments to take action they otherwise might not wish to take. For example, they may have to permit or actively encourage domestic mergers to produce large scale viable domestic alternatives to an incoming company. Political pressures, perhaps based on somewhat nationalistic attitudes, may force the government to oppose the take-over of existing assets by a foreign company. In developing countries this nationalism may express itself in the nationalisation of subsidiaries.

There have been proposals that large multinational companies should be exempt from the coverage of national legislation in regard to restrictive trade practices and some labour provisions. While there might be some grounds for this in some instances, exemption might be conditional on the acceptance of the provisions of ILO conventions or similar minimum standards. The difficulty is that these companies are often of above average efficiency so that the minimum requirement of existing international conventions is really inappropriate; they can afford to meet much higher standards.

The basis of the case for increased government interest in multinational companies is wider than that of trade unions and labour standards, important though these are. Multinational companies extend beyond national frontiers and thereby severely limit the ability of governments, particularly host governments, to adequately control or influence their behaviour. The actions of these companies can be inconsistent with the policies and objectives of individual sovereign states. As governments increasingly adopt some form of economic intervention, or planning, the growth of multinational companies with a corporate objective extending beyond the boundaries of any national policy will lead to friction, and conflicts of interest will be more sharply observed. There is also the danger that irritation with the inability to exert effective economic control within national boundaries will lead to a growth of nationalistic views which would be harmful to the growth of international goodwill. There is always a danger that hostile views will be formed and take a political expression. This is most likely to express itself as anti-Americanism because America has more multinational companies than any other country. But essentially the feeling may really be anti-multinational company; it expresses itself in nationalistic terms because the labels are easier to tag on. It might be better to agree on some form of international rules of behaviour rather than run these risks.

International Organisations

If co-ordinated action by governments is required it is best done through some established international organisation. Trade union organisations, either regional or trade federations could produce guidelines setting out standards of behaviour sought by them. It might be possible to draw up a code of good practice which could be inserted into GATT. Countries could be required to report whether they are observing the conditions, particularly in respect of exports. If this were done, some of the trade unions' fears that companies are moving abroad in order to obtain cheap labour and reduce labour standards would be mitigated. The disadvantages are that the requirements, if they were to have much effect on companies in developed countries, could bear heavily on developing countries, unless double standards were adopted. Also as the obligation for their implementation would rest on governments, trade union organisation and membership growth could be retarded. Trade unions must prefer means which help the development of trade unionism.

There was wide agreement that international organisations have a crucial role to play. Independent organisations such as the OECD could collect facts and analyse the activities of these large multinational companies in an atmosphere where they are not subjected directly to the pressures resulting from attempts to attract investment to a particular place. This allows them to be much more objective. It has been suggested that these companies are often beyond, often thought to be beyond, the effective control of any single government, except possibly that of their parent country. On the other hand, they may be more helpful to a host government with regard to some aspects of policy, e.g. location in developing areas, than domestic companies, as they are internationally mobile and used to setting up new plants they may be less conservative in their location policies.

A study of the companies does not mean that the findings need necessarily be expected to be adverse. Multinational companies might well prove to be more efficient, export more, have faster rates of growth and better records of technological progress than domestic ones. The important thing is to discover the facts in an impartial way. The experience of the OECD in this type of work, and particularly in areas where at the end of the day the co-operation of the participating governments was necessary to achieve action, is especially valuable. Once it is accepted that legislation by individual governments in isolation will not be enough to deal with the problems, the importance of securing agreements between governments is obvious. It was also thought that the OECD experience in labour questions was valuable. If this could be linked with the experience of the Industry Committees which have dealt with similar types of problems it was hoped that effective, detailed and objective studies could emerge.

Recommendation

The group recommended that further work be done in this field. The OECD could collect information about the size and effects of the operations of multinational companies. It was not intended that this be confined to labour questions; the general economic aspects are of vital importance to trade unions and governments. Inter-governmental co-operation through OECD and other international and regional organisations could lead to the acceptance of uniform conditions for the operation of multinational companies, and parent countries too might well agree on general standards of conduct. The experience of OECD in, for example, the Industry Committees where similar types of problems have been studied in the past might prove to be of considerable benefit.

Research could be commissioned to improve our knowledge of the behaviour and characteristics of multinational companies, in particular to discover the site and origin of economic power within these companies, and on their development tendencies. Comprehensive statistical information regarding such things as capital flows, export and import contribution, and profit distribution should be collected, and an assessment of their impact on the various economies made.

CHAPTER 7

Productivity Bargaining

This chapter only attempts to consider briefly some of the features of productivity bargaining and some of the factors responsible for its growth in Britain. It is emphasised therefore that this is neither a comprehensive nor sufficiently deep treatment even of the issues raised.

What is productivity bargaining?

The term was first used by Allan Flanders in his analysis of the developments at the Esso Refinery Fawley.[1]

> The concept of productivity bargaining, as employed in this study, covers any type of collective bargaining in which an increase in the price of labour is associated with an increase in its productivity, regardless of how the latter is achieved. . . . The principle common to all productivity bargaining is the furnishing of an economic inducement for an acceptance of change, but it can be applied to any rules and conventions regulating working practices, including—as in the Fawley example—systematic overtime, job demarcations, the employment of mates, union restrictions on supervision, or procedure for promotion.

A slightly different definition was later provided by the National Board for Prices and Incomes in their first Report on Productivity Agreements;[2] by "a productivity agreement we mean one in which workers agree to make a change, or a

---

[1] *The Fawley Productivity Agreements*, Faber & Faber, London, 1964.

[2] NBPI Report No. 36, Cmnd. 3311, June 1967. This Report, and Report No. 123, contain examples of productivity agreements.

number of changes, in working practice that will lead in itself—leaving out any compensating pay increases—to more economical working; and in return the employer agrees to a higher level of pay or other benefits."

There are some shifts of emphasis between the two definitions but the fundamental concept is the same. Productivity bargaining involves changes in matters affecting the efficient utilisation of labour, which might well also affect other factors of production, which are determined alongside the negotiation of changes in pay or other aspects of the returns to employees. Alternatively we can say that productivity bargaining involves a greater degree of specificity and changes in the conditions surrounding the effort bargain, which are made at the same time as changes affecting the money bargain, and which have the effect of improving the efficiency of labour utilisation in various ways.

The quotation from Flanders mentions the type of changes surrounding the effort bargain or utilisation of labour which might be included in productivity bargaining. Other illustrations can be given. The firm may wish to end the practice of each craftsman having an individual mate (helper); certain craftsmen may carry out only certain tasks and not others which are fully within their capacity and craft training; for historical reasons tasks in one part of the plant may be performed by members of one trade union while identical tasks in a different part may only be performed by members of another union; there may be restrictions on output, or standards of a "fair" day's work imposed by unions or work groups which emanate from past technological conditions; management may have lost effective control over the amount of overtime worked or its allocation; a piecework system may have degenerated as a result of *ad hoc* decisions so that there is now little relationship between effort and reward and no proper incentive effects.

Why productivity bargaining?

It is clear that a necessary pre-condition for productivity bargaining from a management view is that there are areas over which management currently has insufficient or no control affecting the efficiency of labour utilisation and over which it seeks to obtain more control. Thus with an optimum labour force comprised of the technically required skills, performing tasks according to management views of full efficiency with complete management control over the allocation of both work and men and over the number of hours worked and the rates at which they are paid, there would be no opportunity and no economic need for productivity bargaining. This state of affairs seldom, if ever, exists.[3] In the vast majority of cases there are some rules, conventions or accepted practices which result in the under-utilisation or under-employment of resources. These may exist because of formal collective agreements setting out manning scales, job tasks, skill qualifications or other forms of job demarcation, or may be the result of the development of informal workgroup pressures which have effectively imposed unilateral conditions on a work situation, either because new conditions have arisen for which the formal collective agreements provided no agreed solution,[4] or because there has been a gradual encroachment on what might be regarded as traditional managerial authority either as a deliberate policy or as a result of a series of *ad hoc* decisions taken at particular times, possibly in response to acute production problems. In other cases the practices may stem from inadequacies in the pay system or structure. For example, overtime may have come to be regarded as a normal feature and so a part of the workers' pay packet expectations even though it is not currently required for output purposes. Systematic or policy overtime may become built-in to the work situation so that management has lost effective control over the number of hours worked. Alternatively, overtime may have been used to boost the earnings of indirect workers on a time-based payment system in order to maintain some previous differentials in gross earnings which have the sanctity of tradition or equity (often these appear to be the same) behind them, as semi-skilled process workers on payments by results constantly increase their earnings.

---

[3] We are not implying that it should.

[4] Nature in industrial relations as in science abhors a vacuum and if new areas of decision-taking arise someone will step in and take decisions.

Job demarcation or manning scales may owe their origin to tradition or to a particular decision by management taken, perhaps to smooth out industrial problems at a time when there was great pressure to increase output quickly, or to protect certain groups of workers during a temporary downswing in activity. These can become hallowed as custom and practice so that they are no longer subject to managerial control or even to joint regulation through orthodox collective bargaining procedures and practices.

Other practices may result from trade union rules determined on a wider level. For example a craft union may have policies specifying that their members may perform only certain types of work and that other workers may not perform certain tasks. There may be rules, unilaterally determined by trade union policy concerning the use of mates, job content and the type or amount of work it is proper for a member of a particular union or craft to perform. Non-craft unions may also impose conditions, e.g. the T&GWU decided that even though the law had been changed to allow heavy vehicles to run at speeds of up to 40 m.p.h. the conditions of the roads were such that the old legal maximum speed of 30 m.p.h. was to be observed in the interests of safety.

Before management seeks to obtain a productivity agreement it is necessary that it undertakes critical self-analysis. It must decide which areas it needs to obtain control which it does not now have,[5] why it needs that control, and what it is worth in economic terms to obtain it. It is necessary to distinguish those areas or topics over which lack of managerial influence is economically damaging to the firm from those which are irritating to management, perhaps because of status reasons, but may not have any particular economic effect. For example, lack of control over the job content of tasks or the skill demarcation of workers may be economically inefficient. Management may object to the fact that some skilled workers will only accept direct instructions from someone who is qualified in their skill, and it may be irritating to them to be constantly

---

[5] This is not to imply that management can obtain unilateral control over these areas. It will probably secure joint control as is considered below.

reminded that they are not themselves skilled craftsmen, but, depending on the organisational circumstances, this may not have much effect on plant efficiency.

Productivity bargaining removes the protective cloak of alleged union-imposed restrictions on management by creating a margin of opportunity in which management can seek to change those things which are thought to be impeding the efficient running of the plant. No longer can they fall back on workers' restrictive attitudes as a sufficient explanation of inefficiency, as these become negotiable to greater or lesser extent. In this sense the drawing up of a productivity agreement and its successful implementation poses serious challenges to management's own efficiency. It is therefore necessary that management should first acknowledge that there are areas where it has not been able to do those things it wishes and is willing to make concessions in order to be able to exercise greater managerial influence over them. In short, management must know what it wants and why it wants it.

It is perhaps interesting and relevant that the early schemes included British subsidiaries of overseas companies which were concerned at the comparative inefficient utilisation of labour in Britain. Management received an external shock or pressure which pushed them towards productivity bargaining. It is also-interesting that many of the early agreements covered capital intensive operations where labour costs were a relatively small proportion of total costs. However, in these cases, e.g. oil refining, labour costs may be one of the larger elements of *controllable* costs in that they are the main item over which local management can exert influence and therefore become important both as a test of relative managerial ability and as an opportunity for increasing efficiency of production.

The Process of Productivity Bargaining

The particular practices or behaviour patterns which management might wish to change can be considered in different ways which might suggest different types of problems and approaches. One distinction is whether they are internally or externally determined or imposed. Those that result from decisions or developments inside the plant or company are internally determined. The distinction between plant and company is for this purpose primarily to be determined by the coverage of the normal collective bargaining machinery. If multi-plant companies bargain on a plant basis, and seek to continue to do so the plant is the more important unit. Those that arise because of a trade union decision covering all members of the grade etc. should be regarded as externally determined. Thus, while the coverage of the bargaining unit is an important element in deciding whether the practices are internally or externally determined it is not necessarily a sufficient criteria. In some cases the trade union may impose its views irrespective of bargaining units; the T&GWU maximum speed decision and some of the craft rules cut across all bargaining unit boundaries.

Clearly it is more difficult for management, or trade union representatives in a plant or company to change externally-determined rules and conventions. For example, craftsmen may well believe that some of the provisions governing their rules and practices in a plant are not theirs to bargain about; they belong to the whole craft and only the whole craft can agree to change them.

Externally-determined rules or practices are more difficult to change. This is true of all collective bargaining processes; decisions taken outside the coverage of a particular bargaining unit always create additional difficulties if that bargaining unit seeks to change them. The British practice of multi-level bargaining, e.g. industry-wide agreements on some issues supplemented by plant agreements on others, adds to the complications. Because productivity agreements seek to deal with specific practices and obtain specified improvements in efficiency it is more difficult for them to be negotiated on a multi-company basis. Some industry-wide agreements have sought to lay down frameworks within which individual plants or companies can obtain productivity agreements but it is probably the case that for most companies the agreement has to be specifically tailor-made to meet their particular requirements. Multi-plant companies may be able to produce more detailed framework agreements and some agreements in the public sector have gone some way in this respect. An important factor is the degree of uniformity in working practices, production requirements and technology that exist in the various plants or undertakings.

A second important distinction is whether the practices which are to be changed are the result of trade union decisions, either internal or external, or whether they come from action by informal workgroups. Not all practices influencing labour utilisation come from formal trade union decision-taking or bargaining. Indeed they can arise where there are no unions. For example from the viewpoint of labour utilisation and efficiency, there are many companies which could gain advantage by ending the practice of each executive having a private secretary and instituting a secretarial pool system. There are a number of examples where this has been proposed and successfully opposed by the executives who felt they were losing status and privileges.[6]

Informal workgroup practices may raise special problems for collective bargaining in that the official trade union representatives may not be in a position to effectively negotiate changes in them. They may "belong" to groups which do not recognise the right even of their own union to trade them away. Thus, in a number of cases, it is not merely that management has no effective control over the situation, neither have management and trade unions collectively. The processes of bringing these areas under joint regulation therefore requires a tripartite approach. Trade union representatives need to involve workgroups and rank and file members much more than they may feel necessary in ordinary bargaining. Although the usual bargaining over terms and conditions requires rank and file participation the emphasis is mainly on the workers' preferences for the gains to be sought. Productivity bargaining involves changes in working practices and workers' behaviour and they therefore feel much more conscious of the fact that they are being asked to surrender their rights or hard fought for privileges, or protection which they have built up to provide job or income stability. Some of the earlier productivity bargains ran into difficulties because there was insufficient

---

[6] One is tempted to equate this with a craftsman and mate situation but executives, and more frequently their wives, object to secretaries being referred to as mates.

consultation and communication with rank and file in the preliminary stages. If they are not brought into discussion until the main outline and features of the agreement have been settled they are more likely to reject the proposals.

By formalising and specifying agreed conditions in areas which previously had been the result of informal control the nature of the relationships in bargaining will change. In some cases there will be a shift of power from shop stewards acting in an informal manner, e.g. in the allocation of overtime between individuals, to full-time union officials, to trade union branch officials as distinct from shop stewards, or, to the shop stewards officially who will be required to act within a framework of agreed rules. Where, as has occurred in a number of cases, the productivity agreement also involves a change from piecework to a time-based payment system, there may be substantial shifts in power and the processes and content of collective bargaining. In some cases shop stewards have based their considerable power on their ability to negotiate increases in piecework prices as and when the opportunities presented themselves. In a number of plants this may have had relatively little to do with the formal trade union branch structure, particularly where there were a number of trade unions represented in the same plant and inter-union formal co-operation was minimal. The introduction of, say, measured day work removes this traditional power-base of shop stewards. Although they may be formally incorporated into the bargaining machinery, e.g. by representation on committees to discuss job gradings or speeds and feeds this may appear to them as a deliberate attempt to reduce their bargaining strength. In any case it will involve them in abandoning their old skills and they will need to acquire new skills and techniques in such things as job grading and work measurement, which the more militant stewards have regarded as management tools rather than facilities which might aid joint regulation.[7]

The general picture seems to be that shop stewards gain more *formal* power and authority in that they are incorporated

---

[7] The question of power is discussed from the viewpoint of the militant shop steward in *The Employers' Offensive: productivity deals and how to fight them*, Tony Cliff, Pluto Press, London, 1970.

into the agreed procedures and their position and functions set out more clearly. It is less clear whether they actually gain in total effective power in that they generally surrender some of their informal power. Thus the reality may differ from the apparent gains received by stewards which is implied from only a study of the formal procedures. It certainly seems to be the case that in many agreements the lay officers of trade union branches enlarge their role.

There is therefore fair justification for the view that productivity bargaining is about power not money, although money may be necessary to induce the acceptance of changes in existing methods of decision-taking and a re-allocation of the ability to exercise influence or control over a number of areas. At the same time trade unions may gain access to areas of decision-taking over which they currently have no influence. In one agreement dealing with transport workers the decisions on the routing of the delivery lorries was a management right exercised unilaterally, while decisions regarding the timing of runs and the number of deliveries that could be completed in a day was effectively the subject of unilateral control by the workers. As a result of the agreement both questions became the subject of collective decision-taking to a greater extent. This is essentially what productivity bargaining in a Flanders sense is all about; the substitution of joint regulation for uni-lateral control. Management gains control by sharing it, and so do workers. Thus by co-ordinating the money and effort bargains, and by extending the area which is covered by these bargains to include matters which previously either side (or on the workers' side, either the union or the workgroups) controlled unilaterally, there is an increase in the coverage of joint regulation through collective bargaining.

The most telling argument in favour of productivity bargaining is the lack of a practical alternative. It is the only method that promises to be effective in present circumstances in conquering under-employment. The theoretical alternative to inducement is coercion.[8]

---

[8] Flanders, op. cit.

The Growth of Productivity Bargaining

Incomes policy provided a tremendous boost to productivity bargaining. There were various phases of policy under the Labour Government and the criteria and norm changed to reflect the different degrees of severity. The normal basis was similar to the American guideposts with the same four types of exception clauses for wage increases in excess of the norm. For various reasons the three clauses permitting increases for manpower shortages, comparability and low standard of living were seldom successfully invoked by parties appearing before the NBPI. The great weight of exceptional increases was thrown on the productivity clause operative where workers had made a direct contribution towards increasing productivity. During all phases of the policy, but particularly when there was a zero norm, productivity bargaining offered grounds for granting permissible wage increases above the general prevailing level.

The encouragement of productivity-generating settlements was deliberately encouraged on two grounds. Firstly, it was a desirable development in the economy generally; British rates of productivity growth were by international comparisons low. Secondly, the NBPI had to find means whereby it could develop into a positive organisation with a constructive role. The early wage references to the Board tended to be "inquests", i.e. settlements had already been made and the Board was asked to comment on their conformity to policy provisions. Naturally these cases were generally instances where there were *prima facie* grounds for believing that they were in breach of policy. Mere condemnation of these settlements would have relegated the Board to the sterile task of negative critic, and the experience of the recently extinct National Incomes Commission was sufficiently fresh in people's minds to encourage them to avoid this risk of an early demise. The Board therefore adapted its role so that settlements which on the existing terms would have been contrary to policy were made compatible with policy requirements by the addition of productivity-generating changes which justified the above-norm increases. Productivity bargaining was therefore encouraged both by the opportunities provided for higher increases if the negotiating parties could agree on satisfactory changes to increase efficiency and by the post-settlement addition of productivity increases to settlements which would otherwise have called forth condemnation.

In addition the general approach of government was to minimise the restrictive aspects of the policy and encourage a high-wage, high-productivity attitude. The general belief that there was very considerable under-employment and under-utilisation of resources, particularly labour, in the British economy encouraged policy-makers to conclude that this was a fruitful line of economic policy.[9] There was also a growing acceptance in industry that under-utilisation existed and, perhaps more importantly, that something could be done about it. The growing number of companies implementing productivity agreements meant that certain sections of management could no longer blame poor performance on the intransigence of trade unions; they were faced with conditions in which they could be challenged as to their own failures in not resolving some of the problems. The prices side of the policy focussed management attention to cost control and efficiency.

During 1967 there were about 60 agreements a month submitted to the Department of Employment and Productivity for approval on the exceptional ground of a direct contribution by workers.[10] During the first five months of 1968 the average was about 75 a month, and during the rest of that year about 200 a month. During 1969 the figure fell to about 150 a month. By June 1969 some 3,000 agreements had been submitted to the DEP, covering about six million workers, i.e. about 25 per cent of all employed workers.

Currently because of the unusually high unemployment levels there is a marked reluctance by trade unions to make productivity agreements that might have the effect of causing redundancies or reducing job opportunities.

It is probably true that some of the productivity agreements

---

[9] For example the measures of July 1966 which sought to encourage a "shake-out" and re-deployment of labour were part of the same general approach.

[10] This definition is determined by incomes policy purposes and some of these might not normally be considered proper productivity agreements in other circumstances.

signed in incomes policy conditions were more intended to produce acceptable arguments to the policy vetters than to lead to genuine improvements in efficiency. The closing of most doors to wage increases, or above-the-norm increases, other than on productivity grounds, no doubt led to collusive agreements to gloss up a settlement when both sides of industry believed that their own best interests would be served by a wage increase. Such cases will always be difficult to check rigorously as the great bulk of the factual evidence necessary for a proper assessment of the likely outcome of a productivity agreement must come from the parties to that agreement. Incomes policy of the sort Britain sought to apply encourages both genuine and phoney productivity agreements. It is a question of judgement whether the good outweighs the bad. My personal belief is that there was a genuine improvement in attitudes towards productivity-generating changes in this period, which is desirable.[11] The economic consequences of productivity bargaining can be valuable. They can also be undesirable if they lead to situations where no change whatever is accepted unless it is paid for. The crucial distinction comes from the inter-play of the economy-based productivity growth norm and the contribution that can be made by workers making a direct contribution to increased productivity over and above this assessment.

Internal repercussions of productivity bargaining

If productivity bargaining is applied strictly so that only those workers accepting changes in their working practices, job content etc. receive improvements in their conditions there will be repercussions on the existing differentials within the plant. Even if the concept is applied more broadly there are likely to be effects on the broad differentials between blue-collar and white-collar workers. This can raise difficulties. White-collar workers in particular may feel aggrieved if they see an erosion of their relative advantages. The NBPI recog-

---

[11] For a more pessimistic view see *How to Run an Incomes Policy and Why We Made Such a Mess of the Last One*, H. A. Clegg, a former Board Member of the NBPI, Heinemann, London, 1971.

nised very early in its work that it might be impractical to restrict wage increases only to those groups making changes in working practices, and expounded the doctrine of "disturbance allowances" that might need to be paid to other groups to maintain some part, at least, of traditional differentials.[12] Even if there are no incomes policy restraints the question of differentials and the disturbances that might occur as a result of making significant changes in the terms and conditions of some groups of employees will undoubtedly require attention. The difficulty with which this problem can be dealt with will be influenced by the structure and coverage of the bargaining arrangements and units affecting the plant or company. The fragmented nature of much of British bargaining at plant level increases the complexity of the problem.

There is generally a tendency toward increasing formalisation of the workings of the internal labour market and of the rationalisation of wage and salary differentials. Where agreements are linked with reforms of pay systems the importance of this increases. It may be necessary to enlarge the coverage of the fragmented bargaining units which can lead to problems

---

[12] See Report No. 5, "Remuneration of Administrative and Clerical Staff in the Electricity Supply Industry", Cmnd. 2801, October 1965. See also Report No. 123. Agreements covering only one or some groups of workers were referred to as "partial agreements". These "are subject to the risk that managements may be driven to extend pay increases to other workers excluded from their scope with the result that the total increase in costs may outweigh the gains in productivity resulting from the original agreements . . . (Partial agreements) may be useful, provided that they form part of a planned approach and the danger that the benefits will be lost through competitive bargaining and 'leap-frogging' is foreseen and provision made to prevent it". (para. 135(2)). An alternative approach is to include the cost of repercussions in the initial assessment of costs and benefits. By Report 123 the NBPI had switched the emphasis away from the joint regulation views of Flanders to a more efficiency-conscious basis of assessment. This was, of course, the result of the incomes policy requirements they were by statute to observe.

of inter-union rivalries. Moreover the necessity to obtain formal agreement to plant-wide differentials may place additional burdens on trade unions. In a fragmented system they can disclaim responsibility for the resulting structures as they are not formally responsible for the over-all pattern. Thus the internal relationships within trade union organisations might be subject to additional pressures.

Many productivity bargains have involved large upheavals in existing practices and resulted in dramatic revision of wage systems and structures. There has been a tendency to regard them as major exercises which, rightly, take a long period of time to formulate and negotiate. In some situations it might be more appropriate to seek to introduce a process of close and continuing co-operation between management and workers. White-collar workers may not be able to offer substantial "blocks" of changes but may well co-operate in day-to-day adjustments. The NBPI introduced the term "efficiency agreements" to cover the wider variety of continuing co-operation.[13] There is advantage in this additional concept, but also danger that the distinction between additional payment for specific changes and improvements and the basis of ordinary or normal wage levels and increases will become lost.

It is sometimes alleged that if workers agree to a productivity agreement they will be unable to obtain future wage increases unless they are able to continue making changes. There appears to be nothing in the principle of productivity bargaining to lead to this conclusion. Productivity agreements can be seen as additional to what would otherwise have taken place and therefore once an agreement has been made and implemented the parties are free to return to their usual bargaining methods, although it is often the case that qualitatively the actual bargaining after a productivity agreement will be different. The emphasis on joint regulation means that in order to obtain the initial agreement both parties must understand the objectives of the other. They need not agree with them, but if, for example, management does not understand why workers insist on certain provisions, or if workers do not appreciate why management seeks control over manning scales or job content,

---

[13] See Report No. 123.

they are unlikely, in fact, to reach an agreed settlement. By forcing everyone to undertake a deep assessment of the existing situation and decide exactly what it is they want and what they are prepared to do to get it, this type of bargaining imposes a greater degree of reality and recognition of the motives and objectives of the other party upon all concerned.

The increased formality in plant bargaining may bring with it increased rigidity. It may be more difficult to obtain temporary concessions in working rules. However to some extent this might also reduce the possibility of specific decisions becoming translated into general usage by custom and practice. There is a possibility that the letter of the agreement becomes regarded as more important than the spirit.

A common objective of productivity agreements is to reduce the internal boundaries surrounding particular tasks to permit fuller utilisation of resources. Flexibility in manpower allocation and the recognition that a number of different craftsmen might be permitted to perform a multiplicity of tasks which previously had been the prerogative of only some of them, has been much sought after. There have also been occasions on which certain tasks previously regarded as skilled have been recognised as suitable for semi-skilled workers, but there have been difficulties resulting from differences of view as to which specific tasks are semi-skilled and which should continue to remain within the compass of craftsmen. It has generally been easier to obtain relaxations in job demarcations affecting a number of craftsmen where they are each qualified, by their own mutually recognised craft training, to perform the same tasks, than to reach agreement that new workers and particularly semi-skilled ones, should be allowed to perform some of these tasks.[14] Thus craftsmen may agree to recognise the overlapping of skills where these exist and allow a greater degree of transfer but this does not of itself permit "outsiders" to enter the craft demarcation areas. It is similar to the creation of a free trade area; those within it abolish restrictive tariffs or boundaries, but those outside it remain outside faced by the same high wall.

---

[14] The Fawley agreement contained provisions for some mates to be trained to craftsmen.

Economic effects

Critics of productivity bargaining argue that it is immoral or inflationary. The crude equation of this type of bargaining to "buying out restrictive practices" not only ignores the considerable implications for the nature of decision-taking but may encourage the view that it is somehow wrong because it rewards those who have built up restrictive practices in the past and thus have something to sell, whereas those who have co-operated with management in increasing productivity have no opportunity to obtain the particularly large wage increases or improvements on conditions associated with productivity bargaining. It is also argued that workers and unions will be encouraged to create new restrictions in order that they can subsequently sell them.

The immorality argument, in so far as it has an economics content really depends on the money bargain-effort bargain relationships operating in the different plants before and after the productivity agreement. If the "good" plant (without efficiency-restricting practices) was paying the same wages and conditions as the other, that too might be regarded as immoral. If it was paying higher wages (as a simple efficiency-wage concept approach might suggest) then the tendency towards equalisation of wages seems in itself to be neither moral nor immoral. The important point is the relationships prior to the productivity bargain. Similarly if workers are strong enough to impose new restrictive practices on management in order to subsequently sell them, they are presumably also strong enough to press for higher wage increases in any event. Often there is a mixture of economic and institutional argument concerning the processes by which wage increases take place and the effects of each settlement on others running through this type of criticism. The objections can be properly considered only in the full context of events prior to the bargain and an assessment of what is likely to occur if there is, or if there is not, a productivity agreement.

Although it has been frequently alleged that the increases in pay resulting from a productivity agreement will generate pressures for similar increases in other firms in the locality there is little evidence that this has in fact happened.[15] However it may be that there has been pressure for emulation in other firms in the same industry. It does not necessarily follow that the expression of coercive comparisons takes place in local labour markets; it might well be a feature of institutional bargaining arrangements, so that if the usual yardstick for comparability purposes is other firms in the sector irrespective of geographical location, the possible inflationary pressures would be seen outside the local labour market. In fact whether or not these pressures proved to be inflationary would depend on the management response and whether a quoted wage increase in a particular plant obtained by a productivity agreement was matched by a productivity agreement in the second firm. Thus one possibility is that while the results of productivity bargaining might be that some workers quote the high benefits obtained elsewhere the response of management is to press for a productivity agreement in their own plant. In some instances the workers themselves have pressed for a productivity bargain in order to emulate workers elsewhere. As long as the resulting agreements are genuine this can be considered a desirable development.

One way of looking at productivity agreements therefore might be to say that they increasingly isolate the plant from its local economic environment. By concentrating on develop-ments in the internal labour market—and the intention of management is to improve internal efficiency—they weaken such external relationships and comparisons in the external local labour market as may exist. There is thus, for some orthodox economic analysts, a contradiction. The firm is increasing pay, or improving pay and conditions,[16] at the same time that it is reducing its demand for labour. For improve-

---

[15] See NBII Reports Nos. 36 and 123. "The evidence of our case studies bears out the view expressed in Report No. 36—namely, that productivity-based pay increases did not in practice have a direct and immediate effect on the pay rates of other local firms." Para. 105, Report No. 123.

[16] Although standard week or hourly pay may increase substantially there may not be any marked increase in gross earnings if overtime is reduced.

7*

ments in labour utilisation take the form of either reducing the demand for workers of specified skills—e.g. craftsmen if job demarcation rules are relaxed—or of increasing the effective supply of labour of specified skill content from a given number of workers. By removing blockages to the mobility of workers between different jobs, or permitting one craftsman to perform tasks previously requiring two or more different craftsmen, the firm is increasing the supply of labour. The important point is that the firm does this by recourse to the internal rather than the external labour market—although it may require negotiation about rules that are externally determined by a trade union nationally—and so traditional views of the role of wages in attracting or retaining labour from an external labour market position are less important. Indeed as the definitions of productivity bargaining make clear the inducements of higher standard week pay, shorter hours or other improvements in conditions are necessary to persuade unions and workers to accept the efficiency-generating changes. While external labour market conditions might therefore not require improvements in rewards, internal bargaining factors compel an improvement if the desired changes are to be accepted.

Even when productivity bargaining is seen as a response to a particularly tight external labour market which is creating production difficulties as a result of the shortage of certain occupations, the processes by which the firm adjusts to the external conditions is essentially through the internal labour market. It seeks to reduce the number of skilled men it needs to perform a given production requirement by, for example, removing some of the less skilled parts of the current job content of skilled men which can be performed by grades of labour in easier supply, and thereby alters both the demand and supply schedules simultaneously. Improved pay is thus associated with a reduced demand for specific grades of labour because the only way to reduce the demand for that labour—as expressed in the number of men to be employed—is to change the internal work relationships and this cannot be done without the improvements in conditions.

In other cases the abolition of craftsmen's mates might require craftsmen to carry out tasks below their skill capacity but this can lead to considerable improvement in efficiency, particularly if previous practice is for each craftsman to have his own mate. For example at Fawley craftsmen's mates were actually engaged on work only for an average of three-and-a-half hours a day. This unproductive time was obviously very expensive.

There is no reliable statistical evidence available to permit us to decide whether productivity bargaining has had any significant effect in increasing the rate of productivity growth. The pressures of incomes policy probably led to a distortion of the otherwise natural developments. However so long as it is believed that there is significant under-utilisation of labour, pressures to improve efficiency through means analogous to productivity bargaining can be expected to continue.

The conditions in the external labour market will influence trade union responses. Many of the practices which productivity bargaining seeks to remove have developed as a result of trade unions and workgroups searching for additional job and income protection and stability. High employment creates conditions in which this protection can be increasingly obtained from the generally-prevailing economic circumstances, and in recent years this has been buttressed by legislative provisions for redundancy payments and earnings-related social security benefits. The fears associated with measures to reduce the demand for labour as expressed by the number of workers employed in a given plant have therefore been reduced somewhat. However, as unemployment increases, job and income security are sought from internal rather than external sources, and agreements which might involve redundancy or loss of job opportunities to workers currently unemployed are much more likely to be opposed. While there may be greater pressure on firms to obtain productivity agreements in order to reduce costs during times of easing of demand pressures, as competition in the product market intensifies, there is less opportunity to persuade the unions and workers to accept them. Conversely, in times of high demand, firms may feel less motivated to obtain these agreements because of product market conditions, but may feel the pressures of labour market conditions sufficiently acutely to press for them in order to ease their manpower problems. In these circumstances unions may be more willing to enter into productivity bargaining.

Uniquely British?

It is sometimes suggested that the pre-conditions which make productivity bargaining—under-employment or under-utilisation of labour, excessive "policy" overtime and degenerate pay systems—are essentially or predominantly British phenomena so that there is less opportunity, or indeed need, for productivity bargaining in other countries. The absence of multi-unionism in individual plants may also be regarded as providing conditions in which the features of productivity bargaining, e.g. constant assessment of managerial rights, control over manning scales and allocation of labour, are already built-in to bargaining practices, and the bargaining arrangements permit comprehensive plant or company-wide agreements and changes to be negotiated. While there is obviously some weight to this view it is nevertheless probably also the case that in other countries there are restrictions on the most effective economic utilisation of labour which could be reduced by appropriate bargaining. Opportunities may be less widespread and the benefits less dramatic in certain cases but some opportunity exists.[17] An examination of the formal bargaining arrangements may suggest that there is already ample consultation and bargaining about managerial decisions which affect labour utilisation, allocation and efficiency, but in practice the realities of the situation often differ from these formal provisions. Thus while there has been, rightly, considerable emphasis in British comment on the changes in the processes of decision-taking, and in particular the change from unilateral to joint regulation has been emphasised, the potential gains to efficiency should not be ignored. There may be less need to alter the processes of bargaining therefore but still opportunity to obtain improvements in efficiency.

---

[17] Admittedly without great detailed knowledge one is tempted to believe that the US construction industry, or parts of retail distribution, for example, display features appropriate for productivity bargaining.

CHAPTER 8

Forecasting Manpower Requirements: The Functioning of the Labour Market in Practice

Working of the Labour Market

This chapter will be more concerned with the working of the labour market for the more trained, skilled or professional occupations than for relatively unskilled manual workers. First we will look at the factors influencing the demand and supply of particular occupations.

(a) *Demand*

It will be assumed that future demand is given or at least is known or forecasted. It is accepted that this is a very simplifying assumption as future demand may differ from the mere extrapolation of existing trends for the following factors:

(i) a change in product demand, including change in the demand for services, e.g. police or priests;

(ii) a change in technology;

(iii) "institutional", for example manning scales may change, productivity bargaining along British lines may both increase the effective supply of and reduce the demand for certain types of labour within the plant; other changes may not be related to normal collective bargaining but may still influence the demand for labour, e.g. if companies set up central typing pools instead of each executive having his own secretary there may be a reduction in the demand for secretaries;

(iv) there may be deliberate attempts to change labour requirements because of trends in wage costs or because of forecasted shortages. These are to some extent independent of, but to some extent are a reaction to, or caused by, the very existence of manpower forecasting and planning arrangements.

(b) *Supply*

There are essentially two aspects of the supply side that will be considered:

(i) the *potential* supply of trained people, i.e. the number of people who possess (or will possess) the appropriate qualifications at the date in question;

(ii) *actual* supply of people—i.e. the number of people with the appropriate qualifications who are willing, under the conditions existing, to present themselves for employment in the specified occupations on the date in question.

Some of those included under the "potential supply" may in fact not be available as part of the actual supply at the due date as they may choose employment in some other occupation. To some extent this will be influenced by whether their skills are general or specific.[1] Specificity is here used in an occupational sense rather than in the sense of relating to a single employer as is used by Becker. There may thus be wastage of the potential supply to other occupations or employments. It is possible that people will forgo certain quite highly-rated single skills in order to take employment which has a much lower skill level if the attractions are particularly strong.

The Allocation of Labour

The potential supply of labour for a specific occupation can differ from the actual supply. People can choose not to work in the occupation for which they have been trained. If they do so they are in effect deciding to enter some other occupation or to stay out of the labour market altogether, e.g. married women may choose to work in their trained occupation, to work in some other occupation or not to work at all. There are effectively two types of choice open to the worker, firstly, whether to work in the trained occupation, and secondly, in which industry to work, whether in that or in some other occupation. The first question will affect the balance of aggregate demand and aggregate supply for the occupation and the second that of supply and demand by sectors. In order to try and assess the effects of these decisions on labour markets it is

---

[1] See Garry S. Becker, *Human Capital*, NBER, 1964.

necessary to have some explanation of the factors influencing the allocation of labour, and in particular those factors which determine which employments people wish to enter.

The Package Concept

It is clear, and generally accepted, that workers are not attracted or allocated merely by immediate monetary rewards. It is preferable to use a "package" concept so that the reward to labour is seen as comprising three elements; a monetary payment, fringe benefits and "other" attractions. Each of these three items requires further explanation.

Monetary payment is what is generally thought of as wages or earnings. There are difficulties of interpretation in some cases however. Should we compare or consider only wages earned for a standard week, i.e. a constant number of hours worked at non-premium rates, thereby excluding overtime and shift payments? This might seem to be reasonable on the grounds that different payments received as a result of working longer or more inconvenient hours ought not to be regarded as part of the package when contemplating the advantages of different jobs. On the other hand it is now generally accepted that in some occupations or employments in Britain the fact that overtime is available is in itself an added attraction and therefore even though additional hours may have to be worked[2] the extra money received should be taken into account. Certainly employers advertise for labour and draw attention to "opportunities for overtime". This is true in other countries too.

There is also the problem of the time period over which the monetary reward is considered. Incremental salary scales which offer relatively higher pay in the future may be regarded as offsetting relatively low pay for the present or next few years. Is it usual, or even possible to make estimates of life-time earnings?

---

[2] In some cases the hours may not actually be worked but payment may be made; workers might have to be prepared to work the hours actually paid for if the firm requires them to do so.

Fringe Benefits

It is not intended to enter into a discussion of the definition of fringe benefits.[3] It is clear that some fringes are highly regarded by employees and may have a strong recruiting power, e.g. housing in most European countries. Others may have but little, if any, effect on the recruitment of labour, but may help to retain it, e.g. non-transferable company pension schemes. Evidence regarding the retentive effect of non-transferable pensions schemes is in fact relatively small and it appears to suggest that there is less retentive effect than generally supposed. There is almost no limit to the type of fringe benefits a company may provide, although to a large extent the existing government social security provisions play a large part in influencing the type and extent of fringe benefits provided for manual workers. It seems that different fringes exert different attractions to different age groups, and to workers with different personal or family responsibilities. Similarly, the preference for direct money reward or for certain types of fringe benefits seems to be influenced by these factors. There are also the expected differences between the broad groups of manual and white collar workers, with the latter regarding fringe benefits more highly.

To some extent the choice of fringe benefits provided is a unilateral management decision. In Europe there is often less, or no collective bargaining over these issues than is the case with wages. This has important consequences for manpower recruitment and retention. Management may decide to allocate a part of its "total labour cost" on fringes and it is reasonable to suppose that the cost of these to the firm need not be the same as the perceived benefit of them to the workers. It is possible, therefore, for workers to receive either a "surplus" or a "loss" in the relationship between the actual cost of providing the fringes and their perceived benefits. If management wrongly interprets what it thinks its workers want they are in danger of "wasting" that expenditure from a manpower viewpoint. Even if there were collective bargaining with trade unions this danger would remain. It might be less, but it would still be there. For

---

[3] See *Wage Drift, Fringe Benefits and Manpower Distribution,* Derek Robinson, OECD, 1969.

it does not follow that the preferences of the currently employed labour force are the preferences of those workers whom the firm is trying to recruit.

Other attractions

It is extremely difficult if not impossible to quantify these, indeed this is one of the distinguishing features between them and monetary rewards and fringe benefits, (although the latter can also, in some cases, be very difficult to quantify).[4] The more obvious attractions include such things as the environment and atmosphere of the work, the type of person employed in that occupation, family pressures and traditions, the image of the occupation and, as a kind of negative feature, the image and impression of other occupations.

Once the choice of which occupation the worker is to be employed in has been made the second choice, which sector, may be taken on the basis of employment in a particular company rather than in a specific sector or industry. Thus for example, someone may choose to work as a computer programmer. Having made that decision the next choice is more likely to be that of which firm to work for rather than which industry to work in. The choice of the firm effectively chooses the industry and thus determines the distribution of suitably-trained people between different sectors.

In other cases the general conditions of employment in the industry are such that there is relatively little difference between conditions in the various firms. The choice, then, is between an industry and other industries or firms in a number of industries. For example, electricians are qualified to work in a number of industries and may decide that conditions in certain industries, such as construction or shipbuilding, are so unpleasant that they will express clear preferences for employment elsewhere, even though the monetary rewards and fringe benefits are less. Thus, for example, they may forgo a 10 per cent higher wage rather than work outdoor in bad weather or be surrounded by noisy work. In other cases, workers may be reluctant to work in some chemical plants or tanneries because

---

[4] See *Wage Drift, Fringe Benefits and Manpower Distribution*, Chapter III.

of the smells associated with the work. The "other attractions" can be negative; it can then require substantially superior monetary rewards and fringe benefits to attract sufficient labour.

There are decisions taken by people entering the labour force, or preparing to enter the labour force, for the first time, and there are the decisions taken by people already in the labour force, or who have previously been in the labour force, to change their occupation. It is reasonable to suppose that there will be significant differences between the two groups. Initial choices are influenced by a number of factors other than the straight wishes of the individual, e.g. family pressures or advice of school teachers or youth employment officers, and these can be such as to coerce people into training which they subsequently regret. Some indication of this is shown in the different rates of fall-out during training for engineering apprentices which occurs between different towns. What is also interesting is that the fall-out rate during training in some cases does not increase as the number of apprentices increases. It might be expected on some *a priori* grounds that this would occur as increasing the number of apprentices might bring in people who are less "committed" to the occupation and industry.

If trained workers subsequently leave an occupation it follows that forecasts of labour supply can be wrong on the grounds that the actual supply of a specific type of labour will be less than the potential supply, given the relative terms and conditions of that and all other possible alternative employments. If it is accepted that the package concept is an appropriate way of seeking to explain the choice of employment then decisions to leave the occupation for which he has been trained can be the result of a desire to increase monetary rewards or fringe benefits or because of "other attractions".

Downward mobility

There is evidence to show that in certain situations downward occupational mobility can be expected. If a large firm enters an area and pays relatively very high wages to semi-skilled process workers it is probable that some of the more highly skilled workers will leave their trained occupations in order to earn the much higher wages. Examples of this are skilled craftsmen and tradesmen leaving their occupation to work on the assembly line in an automobile factory. The monetary reward is over-ruling the other considerations and is sufficiently positive to offset the strong negative effects of "other attractions" in the process work. Similar results can be seen in respect of some professions which have considerable status, i.e. the "other attractions" are high, but where the money rewards are considered so low that people change to some lower-status but higher-paying job, which might even be non-professional work, e.g. young schoolteachers who become blue-collar workers.

Generalisations are difficult if not impossible, yet it may be that the positive money effect can overcome strong negative "other attractions" effects and draw labour from "higher" occupations, at certain income levels only. Once a minimum income is received the other attractions exert a dominant force. The actual level that is regarded as minimum can change through time and differ from group to group or individual to individual. It could be therefore that there is a mixture of wage levels and wage structure effects. In the case of "downward" mobility (i.e. workers move from an occupation to one that is regarded as less skilled or qualified) which is motivated by money rewards it is necessary that the traditional view of differentials does not hold. Generally speaking we expect wage differentials to reflect skill and training; there are exceptions of course but this is a broad generalisation. However, the mere existence of reversed differentials is not a sufficient condition, it is also necessary that the wage level of the "higher" skilled occupation is regarded as being too low. It is clear that there are many instances of reversed differentials in actual wage levels for different occupations both within a plant and within a local labour market. Significant movement of labour seems to require that workers believe that their own level is too low. It is also possible that even if they do not regard the absolute level in the "higher" skill occupation as too low they might still change their occupation downward if the reversed differential became too wide, i.e. there is some relative difference between wages of two occupations which will induce people to accept downward occupational mobility even if they do not express dissatisfaction with their absolute level of pay. To deny this possibility would be to seek to reject the ultimate basis of economic analysis that *at some level* of differential reward factors of production will become mobile.

So far as actual events are concerned, there is insufficient knowledge of the extent of this downward occupational mobility. We know that it happens but not how much it happens. Nor do we know exactly why. It would be helpful to examine the motives of those who have actually moved downward.

Other mobility

There are two other sorts of mobility so far as an occupation is concerned, sideways, where the person changes occupation by switching to some other of roughly equal skill and standing, and upward mobility, where the worker ceases to be part of the actual supply of that occupation because he is effectively employed in higher-grade work. In both cases the results are the same, there is an effective decrease in the actual supply of the occupation in question below the potential supply as measured by the number of trained people.

Sideways mobility is influenced by the opportunities for such mobility open to the workers which in turn is strongly influenced by whether the skills are general or specific. For example the supply of bus drivers in Britain can be estimated by the number of training opportunities open. There will be some expected sideways loss as qualified drivers leave to drive private coaches. There can also be sideways mobility if the drivers decided to become chauffeurs or lorry drivers. It is true that if all kinds of drivers were looked at together the overall total might not differ, but so far as the sub-groups are concerned, bus drivers can drive cars but ordinary car drivers are not allowed to drive buses without a special licence. Plumbers may move sideways and become heating engineers as the demand for central heating systems increases. In both these cases the moves may be for non-monetary reasons. The bus drivers may prefer more regular hours of work and the plumbers more regular seasonal work and more comfortable surroundings, particularly if they are installing heating systems into houses already built and occupied. The social contact may prove very attractive.

Upward mobility often involves an occupational change, and generally a change away from a narrower specialisation towards more generalised work. This is particularly true of the more professionally trained, e.g. engineers who gradually move over from technical work to general management functions. Unless it has been accepted in the forecasts that part of the demand for general managers will be for trained engineers there will be a loss from potential supply. Mobility can more easily be induced if promotion is offered so that there is a greater probability of "losing" some of the occupation in this way. It is also very difficult to allow for this, for the intake into general management depends on a number of factors besides the initial qualification. There will almost certainly be some imbalance in the forecasts of potential supply of a number of different professional groups as promotions will come from different groups in different amounts. The working of the labour market by attracting labour by offering promotion will therefore often frustrate forecasts of potential supply. One private study in the United States of America showed that over a ten-year period more than half of the number of qualified carpenters ceased working as carpenters. This excludes those leaving for retirement or death and counts as "leaving" skilled carpenters who ceased working at the trade to become foremen or owners of their own businesses other than working-owners.

Evidence concerning the allocation of labour

Such evidence as there is suggests that money rewards are a relatively inefficient or ineffective way of allocating labour. It does not seem to be the case that labour moves towards the higher-paying firm or away from the lower-paying firm, certainly not in the short and medium terms. There is ignorance of the relative conditions existing on the market, and even when knowledge is provided, there is considerable apathy. There is some evidence to suggest that the decision to leave a particular place of employment might be taken before the decision of which alternative employment to accept, indeed the full range of alternatives will often not have been considered before taking the decision to leave, and may not be reviewed afterwards either.

This implies that those firms seeking to attract labour must push their vacancies to the forefront of the attention of those seeking a job, or those who might be induced to change work. General experience is that for blue collar workers word-of-mouth recommendation by a friend is one of the most common forms of introduction of labour. This is one way of overcoming the bad image that the firm or industry may have. In many cases peoples' views of the nature of certain jobs must be based on images given them by others; they cannot possibly have personal experience of all the jobs open to them. Labour will be *attracted* therefore, by the image that a firm, occupation or industry has, although once recruited it will be *retained* according to the experiences of the job situation in the widest sense.

Types of situation

The previous very sketchy discussion of certain features of the labour market as they might affect manpower allocation permits us to consider a few situations in more detail.

(a) Aggregate supply and demand in balance but imbalances between sectors. Even though the overall forecasts might prove accurate it is possible that the allocations between sectors is distorted. There is evidence to show that wage structures vary from industry to industry, and indeed from plant to plant. If workers react to wage levels and relative wage levels they will tend to move to some sectors and not others. Internal wage structures may be sufficiently sticky to prevent the adjustment necessary to correct this. If labour is less responsive to changes in relative wages it may be that the less tangible attractions are insufficient to induce labour to move or that the labour concerned does not know what those attractions really are. It may be very difficult to do anything about this for if different groups react to different mixes of components in the package and prefer different absolute levels of different items, then the package of attractions that is most suited to the majority of the employees may be ill-suited to the demands of specific occupations. The institutions of the internal labour market may then make it extremely difficult to change the package for a minority. In these circumstances the firm, or industry, may be unable to compete effectively for labour on the existing external markets.

One possibility is to turn to the internal labour market and effectively decrease the demand for that sort of labour or increase the supply by internal training and promotion etc. This will lead to an imbalance in the aggregate, but this is not a matter of great concern to the individual firm.

One reason for the imbalances is that the working conditions for members of the same occupation can vary considerably from industry to industry. Conditions in the construction industry are often unpleasant and imply that employees spend a fair amount of time in the open. This may or may not prove attractive to, say, qualified engineers or technicians. In other cases conditions are so attractive that there is an excess of supply at prevailing market rates, e.g. secretaries in the film and television industries. Essentially, this is because there are two factors at work, (i) a decision about the occupation to be followed, and (ii) a decision about the place of work, firm or industry, in which that occupation is to be practised. These two decisions may be closely linked, but in other cases they are not. It is, on the whole, easier to forecast either one of these than both. Labour market pressures affect both decisions but may not do so equally, or even in the same direction. This depends on people's preferences for intangibles, for the monetary aspects and fringe benefits are only part of the total attraction of labour to specific places of employment.

(b) *Aggregate supply and demand are not in balance*

There are two possibilities; demand can exceed supply and demand can be less than supply.

Excess demand. Four lines of action are open to the firm or industry in situations where the demand for a particular occupation exceeds supply.

(i) Intensify competition for existing supply of the occupation. This will generally involve increasing pay, advertising and offering such incentives as seem likely to attract the type of labour concerned, e.g. provision of housing, payment of educational fees for children etc.

(ii) Expand the frontiers limiting supply. This depends on the type of occupation and the length and type of training required. A firm may seek to increase the effective supply *to itself* by internal training or by inducing qualified workers to re-enter the labour force thereby increasing the potential supply, e.g. the provision of creches may permit married women to return to work much sooner than planned, or the provision of shift working may permit part-time working.

(iii) Turn to the *internal* labour market. This is often the first response as longer hours of work are called for. Other possibilities include internal training and promotion which increase the effective supply and changes in manning scales and working arrangements which have the effect of decreasing demand. For example, productivity bargaining which ends the practice of every craftsman having his own mate and provides for craftsmen to be employed more flexibly on different kinds of work does both of these things. The creation of a pool of secretaries to replace a system where every executive has his own reduces the demand for secretaries. In other situations the recruitment of higher-grade secretaries can allow scarce managerial talent to rid itself of relatively minor tasks and concentrate on the duties most appropriate to its abilities. This is one of the general responses to scarcities. The job tends to become redesigned to permit the qualified workers to concentrate on those aspects of work which really require their skills.

A variation of the same approach is to recruit less skilled workers thereby effectively redesigning the job so that occupations with the same name will cover different skill contents.

(iv) By opting out of the labour market the firm may avoid the pressures of shortages, e.g. plant can be located in geographical areas where the shortages are less acute or the work can be "farmed out", e.g. some American companies have opened offices in Europe where draughtsman's work is done.

In this tight labour market workers will then tend to choose the composition of the package most attractive to them and not respond to monetary rewards alone. The large number of job opportunities open to workers permits them to exercise their preferences and the promotion prospects to fill vacancies will lead to an increase in mobility. Some occupations and sectors will be affected more than others. If, at the same time, there have been shifts in the underlying images and tasks, so that some sectors have become more unpopular (i.e. the "other attractions" have a strong negative effect), some sectors will have persistent shortages. Moreover these may express themselves in occupations for which no initial shortage was felt.

Occupational mobility can have the effect of shunting the shortages downward to some "port-of-entry" occupation.

Excess supply

In an economy generally regarded as being fully employed there can be an excess supply of a particular occupation for two main reasons:

(1) A temporary reduction in demand due to fluctuations in product demands. Often firms will take a longer-term view and hold on to the workers, particularly if they are skilled and usually in short supply. Sometimes these workers may be temporarily down-graded or put on to work with a lower skill content.

(2) A permanent reduction in demand due to changing technological or institutional factors. In this case there is a stock of workers who will not be able to obtain employment in their trained occupation. There are three main methods of response.

(a) The workers will accept lower-skilled employment which might utilise some of their skills. In other cases there may be no demand for their lesser skills so that they have to accept quite unskilled employment.

(b) Upward mobility may be possible depending on the training facilities available. Full employment economies are subject to constant change; the demand for some occupations falls and rises for others. The pressures of adaptation can be such as to provide aids to retraining.

(c) The internal labour market can absorb the excess supply, either by returning or by downgrading with "bumping". Thus workers in excess supply may claim seniority rights so that the workers actually put on to the external labour market as unemployed are junior and less skilled. The institutional conditions of the internal labour market will be crucial determinants of the extent and form of effects on the external market. Similarly, the industry may provide training in order to retain the surplus occupation, thereby passing on the pressure to some other occupation. It is often a condition of acceptance of technological change by trade unions that retraining facilities be provided for those made redundant.

It is not possible to be precise about the exact way in which surplus labour will be absorbed. The degree of specificity of the skills will have some effect on determining whether the surplus workers move upwards or downwards occupationally, but institutional factors can be of overriding importance. Workers will be exercising some choice regarding entering a new occupation, but this choice differs from the casual choice of occupation. If the degree of labour surplus is marked other employers may make deliberate efforts to recruit. For example, if there is large-scale redundancy, employers who are short of labour in other occupations may seek to recruit in order to train them to meet particular shortages elsewhere.

INDEX

Advisory Council on Economic and Social Problems, 17–18
American multinational companies, 163, 164, 170
American Steelworkers Union, 177
arbitration, 23, 61–3, 66
attitudes: to capital sharing, 95–102, 148; to German capital sharing plans, 117–22; to incomes policies, 13–14, 37, 75
Austria, 14–22; establishment of prices and incomes machinery, 21; lack of official policy, 18; Sub-Commission on Wages, 16–17; Sub-Committee on prices, 15–16; trade unions, 21

balance of payments, 143–4, 181
banks, 122, 133–4
bargaining, see collective bargaining
Britain, see United Kingdom
British Wages Councils, 63
Burgbacher Plan, 89, 116

Canadian Trades Union Congress, 175
Capital Advisory Council on Economic and Social problems (Austria), 15
capital flows, 180
capital growth sharing, 77, 78–81; favoured by trade unions, 97, 102
capital sharing schemes, 76–104, 137–157; and incomes policies, 119, 145–150; control of funds, 83; criticism of, 102; Denmark, 90–2; France, 92–5; economic arguments against, 143–4; Germany, 88–9; inflationary results of, 86; Italy 89–90; motives for, 83–6; Netherlands, 87–8; participation in, 83; trade union attitudes to, 95–104; types of scheme, 97–8; see also workers' savings plans

collective bargaining: and arbitration, 62; and incomes policies, 43, 68–9; and income redistribution, 139; at plant level, 47; in the public sector, 68; Germany, 105; international, 175–9; intervention in, 58–60; investment wages, 77–8; Ireland, 33–4; multinational companies, 166, 168–169; over fringe benefits, 208; productivity bargaining and, 190
collusion between unions and employers, 60–1, 151, 196
Comité Arbeitersnacht (Netherlands), 40
companies: capital sharing schemes, 141; liquidity, 98; passing on cost increases, 152; productivity bargaining in, 185–207; passim; see also employers and multinational companies
comparability and wage claims, 63–7; importance of, 66; in the public sector, 64
conflict: about take-overs, 174; and multinational companies, 163; between arbitration and incomes policy, 61–3; between countries, 180; between employers and labour, 26; between government departments, 57; between national trade unions, 178; between public and private interest, 71; between union leaders and rank and file, 27, 49; between redistribution and investment, 140; between wage and salary earners, 48–9
construction industry (Germany), 138
consumer boycotts, 177
consumption and capital sharing, 126, 139, 148, 150
cost increases, 15, 152
cost of living, 32

219